CHRIST CRUCIFIED

This book belongs to

IAN ANDERSON'S

CHRIST CRUCIFIED

AND OTHER MEDITATIONS
OF A DURHAM HERMIT

edited and introduced by

David Hugh Farmer

translated by

Dame Frideswide Sandeman O.S.B.

Gracewing.

CHRISTIAN CLASSICS

First published in 1994

Gracewing
Fowler Wright Books
2 Southern Ave, Leominster
Herefordshire HR6 0QF
United Kingdom

Christian Classics
PO Box 30
Westminster
Maryland 21157
USA

Distributed

In New Zealand by
Catholic Supplies Ltd
80 Adelaide Road
Wellington
New Zealand

In Australia by
Charles Paine Pty
8 Ferris Street
North Parramatta
NSW 2151 Australia

Typesetting courtesy of Darton, Longman & Todd, and Reesprint, Radley, Oxfordshire

Printed by Progressive Printing (U.K.) Ltd., Leigh-on-Sea, Essex.

UK ISBN 0 85244 266 1
US ISBN 0 87061 202 6

CONTENTS

LIST OF ABBREVIATIONS

CS=Camden Series
SS=Surtees Society
PL=J.P. Migne, *Patrologia Latina*
RS=Rolls Series
DB=H. Denzinger and J. B. Umberg, *Enchiridion Symbolorum*
JBAA=*Journal of the British Archaeological Association*

PREFACE

The meditations printed below, written by a fourteenth-century monk of Durham who became a hermit on the island of the Inner Farne off the Northumberland coast, were for long unpublished and virtually unknown. Although James Raine, canon of Durham, had drawn attention to them in 1852, credit for their modern rediscovery belongs to W.A. Pantin (of Oriel College, Oxford), who described them and printed some extracts in 1944. In 1957 the present writer published the Latin text in full, following this up with an English edition in 1961, with the title *The Monk of Farne*. Renewed interest in this personal and monastic work, aroused both by its intrinsic quality and by recent studies on Durham Priory and on other mystics of the same period, has made a new edition desirable. It is believed that it will appeal to many English-speaking readers of today.[1]

A monastic hermit might seem to many a contradiction in terms. St Benedict legislated for the 'strong race of cenobites'; that is, community monks, and emphasised frequently the importance of community virtues like obedience and fraternal charity. At the same time, as a follower of eastern and western monastic tradition, he esteemed the solitary life as something to be followed after years of probation in the monastery, as a more difficult vocation to 'single combat with the devil'. This idea was widely accepted in both East and West, not least in medieval England. Records of English hermits and anchoresses show that the practice of the solitary life was widespread. Not a few of these had been members of Benedictine, Dominican or Augustinian monasteries first; several Benedictine abbeys provided for a hermitage to be occupied within their churches, including Durham. Julian of Norwich, the best known of the English Mystics of the fourteenth century, may well have been a Benedictine nun before becoming an anchoress.

Durham itself had shown special interest in the hermit life for a very long time. Since its establishment as a monastic cathedral in 1083 it had incorporated within its ambit the historic centres of Northumbrian Christianity: Lindisfarne, Wearmouth, Jarrow and the Farne islands. All of these were closely linked

with two of the greateſt Anglo-Saxon saints Bede and Cuthbert. The relics of both were buried in Durham's Galilee chapel,
and both inspired generations of Durham monks by their sanctity. This was seen in the biblical and hiſtorical works of Bede
and in the more varied monaſtic life of Cuthbert, who was in
turn, cenobite, hermit and bishop. Too easily is it forgotten that
Cuthbert was a bishop only for the laſt two years of his life. Had
he died in 685 inſtead of 687, he would have been venerated as
a monk inſtead of as a bishop. This moſt popular of northern
saints, twice 'promoted' from ordinary monaſtic life, died as a
hermit on the Inner Farne, to which he had retired knowing
that his death was near. He was aged only fifty-three.[2]

Durham was and is especially Cuthbert's city. The Durham
monks were miniſters of Cuthbert and the cuſtodians of his
long-incorrupt body, verified as such in 698, 1104 and 1539. The
properties they owned were called the patrimony of St Cuthbert. The works of art in the cathedral and the books in the
library witness to the abiding intereſt and devotion of this community to their patron. It was therefore not surprising that a
series of Durham monks became hermits on the bleak Farne
islands, but they were always a tiny minority compared with
those who ſtayed in the diſtinguished but comfortable milieu
of the cathedral or else spent part of their lives in one or other
of Durham's solitary houses.[3]

It will be shown below that there were sound reasons for
identifying the author of these meditations with John Whiterig, a monk of Durham from *c.* 1350 until his death, probably
on Farne in 1371, at about the same age as Cuthbert and on the
island sanctified by his patron. The final meditation in the sole
surviving manuscript of these works is dedicated to Cuthbert
and breaks off unfinished. Fortunately he had finished the other
meditations already.

The principal one is on Chriſt Crucified. This is easily the
longeſt as well as the moſt important. It is deeply inspired by
the texts of the Bible and the Liturgy. It is traditional, personal
and affective. It is a document of its own time, but also has a
timeless character. This is why it appeals to people of our own
age.

Although we know few of the facts of the author's life, we

can relate to him as one who was cheerful in auſterity, warm-hearted in his learning and utterly committed to his way of life. Sensitive to the beauty of nature and to the work of divine grace in the souls of men, he lived long enough to express in writing the deepeſt conviƈtions of his life. For him the love of God was paramount, giving meaning to monaſtic life, whether lived in community or in solitude.

Notes to Preface

1. J. Raine, *The Hiſtory and Antiquities of North Durham* (1852), 359–60; W. A. Pantin, 'The Monk-Solitary of Farne: a Fourteenth-century English myſtic', *English Hiſtorical Review* May 1944, 162–86; D. H. Farmer, 'The Meditations of the Monk of Farne', *Analeƈta Monaſtica* IV (1957), 141–245, *The Monk of Farne* (Darton, Longman & Todd, 1961).
2. For Durham see D. Knowles, *The Monaſtic Order in England* (Cambridge, 1966), 164–71, 622–30; *The Religious Orders in England* II (1979), 313–28; and especially R. B. Dobson, *Durham Priory 1400–1450* (Cambridge, 1973), 11–50 and *passim*; Bede's *Life of St Cuthbert* is translated in *The Age of Bede* (ed. J.F. Webb and D. H. Farmer, Harmondsworth 1988), 41–102.
3. Dobson, *op. cit.*; D. H. Farmer, *The Oxford Diƈtionary of Saints* (third ed. 1992), 116–8. See also *St Cuthbert, his Cult and Community to AD 1200* (Woodbridge, 1989), edited by G. Bonner and others.

Introduction

I. THE MANUSCRIPT

In the library of the Dean and Chapter of Durham, which contains the best collection of medieval monastic manuscripts to survive *in situ* in this country, is a fifteenth-century Latin manuscript book (B. IV, 34) of quarto size containing works of spiritual theology written by Durham monks of the fourteenth century. It consists of three parts of different date.

The first five leaves contain a series of mnemonic verses about the antiphons of the Divine Office in a mid-fifteenth-century hand; ff. 6–75v (originally numbered 1–71v) contain the meditations translated below: after four blank leaves there follow on ff. 80–115v, two treatises on the monastic life (still unprinted) by the famous Durham monk Uthred of Boldon entitled *De substancialibus regule monachalis* (f. 80) and *De perfeccione uiuendi in religione* written in a hand of *c.* 1400.[1]

Here we are concerned only with the second part of this manuscript. Written in a very good hand of the late fourteenth century, it probably existed first as a separate book and was bound up later with the other works, which are written in different, later and less elegant hands. Headed *Meditaciones cuiusdam monachi apud Farneland quondam solitarii*, it contains seven meditations in all, addressed respectively to Christ Crucified, to our Lady, the Angels, Abraham and David, St John the Evangelist (2), and St Cuthbert (incomplete). The first is the most important and is longer than all the others put together. Originally the scribe divided the text into thirty long paragraphs with a coloured capital at the beginning of each; afterwards he subdivided the text into chapters, headed by the mark ¶ in red in the margin together with the number of the chapter. In this last process he omitted six numbers by mistake, so that in the manuscript the meditation to Christ Crucified appears to contain 104 chapters instead of 98. This subdivision into chapters does not always correspond exactly with the author's thought, and this, together with the presence of scribal errors most easily explained by misreading another manuscript, seems to indicate that our manuscript is not the author's auto-graph.[2] It could, however, have been copied directly from the autograph. Punctuation consists mainly of full stops only at the end of each sentence.

The pages measure 6¼″ by 9¾″ and the text occupies a space 5″ by 8¼″. There are 22–27 lines per page. There are very few corrections, all in the scribe's own hand. At the top of the first page above the title (f. 6 in the modern numbering) is the inscription in another hand *Liber Petri de Dunelm' monachi eiusdem.* A Peter of Durham occurs in the Durham *Liber Vitae* (f. 69v) under the year 1345; if this was the same person, he would have been some years senior to the author. The presence of his name here indicates neither that he was the author nor the scribe of the book, but simply its owner.

When the three parts of the whole manuscript B. IV, 34, had been assembled, a list of contents was added on what is now f. 5v. This scribe (of *c.* 1400) concluded his list with the following lines:

> *In meditacione mea exardescit ignis.* (Psalm 38, 4.)
> *Meditacio mortis summa prudencia.*†

After Uthred's second treatise followed by four lines headed *Holcot Super Sapienciam* the same scribe added the couplet:

> *Viuere quisque diu querit, bene uiuere nemo:*
> *Et bene quisque potest uiuere, nemo diu.*‡

His recording of such thoughts may serve to conclude this section.

II. THE AUTHOR

The title of the manuscript tells us that the author was a monk who lived as a solitary at Farne. Since 1255 this island of the Inner Farne had become a regular cell of Durham, which generally housed two monks, the Master and his companion. Hence it is clear that the author was a monk of Durham. From the meditations themselves we also know that he had studied at Oxford (p. 134) and that he wrote at least one of his medi-

---

†In my meditation the fire is kindled (Psalm 38,4.)
　Meditation on death is the highest prudence.
‡Everyone seeks to live long, none to live well;
　Yet everyone *can* live well, but none can live very long.

tations after a serious outbreak of plague (p. 147). The Black
Death visited England in 1349 and again, with greater effect on
the records, in 1361–2, 1368–9 and 1371.

From the author's language about St John the Evangelist we
can infer that his name was John. In his second meditation to
this saint he recognizes that he himself is specially entrusted to
St John, that St John is his patron and a special inspiration to
him, and deserves to be loved above all other saints except our
Lady, more even than St John the Baptist, who was tradition-
ally regarded as the special patron of monks in general, and of
hermits in particular.

Now only two Durham monks called John are known to have
lived on Farne in the second half of the fourteenth century: John
Abell, formerly Chamberlain at Durham, Master of Farne 1357–
8 and the first whose accounts have survived, and afterwards
Bursar at Durham. There is no suggestion that he ever lived as a
solitary, his monastic career clearly lay in the line of finance and
administration, and it seems much more likely that our author
should be identified with the Dom John Whiterig who died at
Farne in 1371, when 13*s* 4*d*. was given from there to the poor
in alms for his soul, and 10*s*. given at Durham for the same
purpose.[3] Whiterig, whose name is also spelt Quitrig, Quitrik
or Whitriggs, was never Master but was socius of Farne, but
there is reason to suppose, as will be shown below, that he was
for some years previously master of novices at Durham, which
fits in well with the spiritual character shown by the author of
these meditations.

It seems certain that Whiterig was a Northerner: his name
indicates the place of origin of his family. This could be identified with White Ridge in Cumberland on the banks of Wothen-
pool or perhaps with Wheatridge in Northumberland. It is also
interesting to note that Bishop Hatfield's Register records that
a John Whytrick of Darlington incurred major excommunica-
tion for a crime of violence against the chaplain John of Eastry
on 23rd April 1355, and was absolved from it on 9th May following.[4] This person cannot be identified with his namesake,
for our John Whiterig first occurs in the Durham records in
the *Liber Vitae* (f. 69v), as the first of a group of ten monks, in
1353. This means that he was certainly a monk of Durham by

this date, and probably before, because the scribes of this book seem sometimes to have waited for a few years before writing in quite a long list of names at a time, as on the very next page.

His name, however, occurs neither in the remarkably full ordination lists of 1333–40 nor in the list of 82 Durham monks recorded in Richard of Bury's Register in the year 1342.[5] Neither is a John Whiterig found in the documents concerning the election of John Fossor as prior in 1341 nor those of Hatfield's election in 1345. Hence Whiterig was not a monk of Durham by 1345. The surviving lists of monks from Durham College, Oxford, date from a time long after his death, so it has not been possible to trace him there either. All that we can say for certain about the date of his entry into the monastery is that it was between 1345 and 1353.

Although owing to the longevity of both Fossor (d. 1374) and Hatfield (d. 1381) Whiterig never took part in an election, certain details about his life have been gleaned from the Durham Obedientiary Rolls. His name occurs in the Chamberlain's Rolls in the same entry as the novices in the years 1356–7, 1357–8 and 1358–9 as follows:

1356–7. Item in xvi paribus botarum emptis pro nouiciis et Iohanne Qwitrik et uno pari pro camerario, xix s. viii d.

1357–8. Et in xix pellicibus pro nouiciis et Iohanne de Qwitdrik cum ix coopertoriis pro lectis et ix fururis, vii l.

Et in xxi paribus botarum emptis pro eisdem nouiciis, Iohanne de Quitrik et camerario, xxxii s. ix d.

1358–9. Et in x pellicibus emptis pro nouiciis et Iohanne de Whitriggs, xxii s.

Et in xxi paribus botarum emptis pro nouiciis, Iohanne de Whitriggs et camerario, quarum x fuerunt linata, xxvii s. vi d.†

†1356–7. Item for 16 pairs of boots bought for the novices and John Quitrik and one pair for the Chamberlain: 19*s*. 8*d*.

   1357–8.

     And for 19 skins for the novices and John of Quitrik with nine covers for their beds and nine furs: £7.

     And for 21 pairs of boots bought for the same novices, John of Quitrik and the Chamberlain: 32*s*. 9*d*.

   1358–9.

     And for 10 skins bought for the novices and John of Whitriggs: 22*s*.

     And for 21 pairs of boots bought for the novices, John of Whitriggs and the Chamberlain of which ten were lined: 27*s*. 6*d*.

For the next four years the Chamberlain's Rolls have not survived, but in 1363–4 Whiterig appears for a small money payment, but apart from the novices. By this time he was already on Farne, but he continued to receive a payment of 17*s*. or 18*s*. each year. This item moves from year to year from one section of the roll to another, sometimes under the general heading *Expensa lanarum et linen'*, and sometimes under the general heading *Expensa Nouitiorum* which actually includes other non-novitiate items too, but never, as in 1356–9, sharing the same entry as the novices. It seems probable that a hermit did not fit tidily into any single category, and the accountant therefore adopted divergent practice in accounting for his expenses.

From the year 1363 until 1371 John Qwitrig's name appears in the annual accounts of Farne, either by name (1363, 1364, 1365, 1368) or described as *socius*, generally for a payment of 13*s*. 4*d*. This payment would presumably have been made for small necessaries like parchment and ink and other few out-of-pocket expenses, while the money provided by the Chamberlain would have been for clothing. In the year of Whiterig's death (1371) there occurs the final mention of him in the Farne Rolls, when the money payment made habitually to him was given to the poor instead: *Et in distributione facta in cibariis datis pro anima domini J. de Whiterig*, xiii s. iv d.†

From the various data provided by the Rolls the following chronology, very incomplete, may be suggested:

c. 1350. Became monk at Durham, studying at Oxford either before or after.

1353. Visit to Farne (5*s*. entered in the Bursar's Roll for this purpose).

1356–7. Visited Farne again, receiving 6*s*. 8*d*. there (Farne Rolls), possibly a trial period.

1356–7. Became Novice-master, remaining in office certainly until 1359 and possibly until 1363.

1358–9. Visited Lindisfarne (5*s*. entered in the Bursar's Roll for this purpose).

---

†And for the distribution of food made for the soul of Dom J. of Whiterig: 13*s*. 4*d*.

1363. Settled at Farne. In this year a new house was built there
   costing £3 7s. 8d. (Farne Rolls), which may have been destined for him.

1371. Died at Farne, presumably after continuous residence
   there since 1363, during which he wrote the meditations.
   After less than 25 years of monastic life, he would probably
   have been aged about fifty.

Whiterig represents the spiritual aspirations of the simple
monks of the cloister rather than the obedientiaries. He never
held an obedience which involved temporal administration, and
his writings form a useful corrective to the impression gained
by too exclusive a concentration on financial records. If few
monks wrote such meditations, very many must have shared the
outlook and scale of values of their author. And these writings
are more revealing about how the monks actually prayed than
are treatises on how prayer should be made. We may, however,
regret that Whiterig died perhaps before he attained his full
spiritual development.

III. The Milieu

John Whiterig's life was passed during an eventful period
of English history. During the greater part of it Edward III
was king of England. There was intermittent warfare with the
Scots from 1327–8 and again from 1332 until the beginning of the
Hundred Years War in 1337. These events all affected Durham
closely. Some years before Whiterig became a monk, soon after
the battle of Crecy, the famous battle of Neville's Cross was
fought just outside Durham in 1346, when king David II of
Scotland, to relieve pressure on the French, had invaded England with a large army. He was decisively defeated and taken
prisoner by an English army under queen Philippa, assisted
by archbishop Zouche of York, which was largely composed
of Northern levies which the prior of Durham had helped to
raise.[6] A precious trophy of the battle was the famous Black
Rood of Scotland, a blackened silver crucifix which had come
from Holyrood and which remained in the south alley of the
choir of Durham cathedral until the Reformation.[7] Of less
immediate concern to Durham was the battle of Poitiers in
1357, but the capture of the French king there led to the treaty

of Calais in 1360 and eventually to a ten years' truce with Scotland which lasted until Whiterig's death.

In the life of the Church as a whole these years were no
less eventful. Since 1309 the popes had been resident at Avi-
gnon, and this so-called Babylonian Captivity did not end until
1378. Church-State relations were the subject of direct conflict
between pope and emperor on the Continent, while in England each side manoeuvred for position, avoiding open conflict:
on the one hand anti-papal agitation led to the passing of the
Statutes of Praemunire and Provisors, while on the other hand
king and pope in practice came to terms with each other and
found a *modus vivendi*.

Doctrinal controversies were also numerous. At Oxford,
where Whiterig studied in his youth, seculars and mendi-
cants were at odds over questions such as dominion and grace,
while later in the century John Wyclif emerged as the most
important unorthodox theologian of his day in England and all
the religious theologians joined forces against him, especially
against his heretical teaching on the Eucharist.[8] One of his
most important opponents was Uthred of Boldon (*c.* 1324–97),
monk of Durham, an influential doctor of theology of Oxford
University, until some of his views on grace and predestination
were condemned by archbishop Langham in 1368. None the
less he is considered by modern writers to be the fourteenth
century's most notable monk-graduate. Uthred would doubt-
less have known Whiterig, but as most of his earlier years were
spent in Oxford, while Whiterig had retired to Farne by the
time Uthred returned to the North, they would probably not
have had close continuous contact with each other.[8a]

Although the fourteenth century was a time when subversive
theories on grace, the sacraments and papal jurisdiction came
to their full development, more orthodox movements also
flourished. Both in England and on the Continent mystical
writings were produced which in quantity and in quality were
surpassed by those of no other century of the Middle Ages.
In England, too, there was a notable revival of the monastic
life. Hermits were numerous, the Carthusians increased their
monasteries from two to seven, while some of the great Benedi-
tine monasteries, including Durham, recovered rapidly from
the Black Death. At least five Benedictine monks occupied

important positions to which no parallel can be provided by the thirteenth century: Simon Langham, archbishop of Canterbury and cardinal, Adam Easton, bishop of Norwich and cardinal, Thomas Brinton, a saintly predecessor of St John Fisher in the see of Rochester, Uthred of Boldon, already mentioned, and Thomas de la Mare, abbot of St Albans and so successful in his visitations of other Black Monk monasteries that he was known as their *patriarcha* even at Rome. The lives of such men, together with the spiritual writings of the period, some still largely unexplored, the developments in art, architecture and administration and the increase of personnel, all point to a very real Benedictine revival in fourteenth-century England. In their relations to the outside world also the Black Monk monasteries of the later Middle Ages tended to increase rather than decrease in importance.[9]

Durham in particular was fortunate at this time. John Fossor, elected prior on 16th March, 1341, a learned and eloquent man, received to profession 120 monks during his reign of thirty-three years, if we may believe the testimony of the Durham domestic chronicler. He was also responsible for the two new windows in the North and South transepts of Durham cathedral, to which he also made many gifts of vestments and statues. He was an excellent administrator too, paying off old debts and putting up new buildings, while a further indication of the good rule and financial order of the house is the surviving series of Obedientiary Rolls. He was the first prior of Durham to be buried within the cathedral. Fossor had granted a similar privilege to Ralph and Alice Nevill, outstanding friends and benefactors of the community, who enriched the cathedral with the beautiful stone reredos of delicate Perpendicular tabernacle work, which still stands behind the High Altar and is known as the Nevill screen.[9a]

Although the Black Death occurred during Fossor's rule, the first visitation by bishop Hatfield soon afterwards showed that Durham had quickly recovered from this disaster. Hatfield, previously keeper of the king's privy seal, was consecrated to the see of Durham in 1345, and, in spite of his enemies' accusation of insufficient learning, not only left a gracious memory behind him for magnificence, generosity and accessibility to the monks but also adequately endowed their college at Oxford.

The new bishop's throne he built in his cathedral over a splendid tomb is reputed to be the highest in Christendom.[10]

Perhaps Durham had never enjoyed so much temporal prosperity as at this time. And it may have been in reaction against this that Whiterig chose to live in the grim austerity of the Inner Farne. He was also probably out of sympathy with certain of the monk-graduates: he criticizes monks who were religious only in name, but were still through lack of generosity attached excessively to what they should have renounced (p. 90-1); but there is no reason to suppose that such were the majority of the Durham community. The mere fact of the continuance of the eremitical tradition at Farne and even, perhaps, in an anchorage in the cathedral itself, together with the patronage of and frequent gifts to neighbouring hermits by priors of Durham, point rather to the survival of the fervour of twelfth-century Durham into the fourteenth.

In choosing the life of a hermit John Whiterig followed a slight but persistent tradition among Benedictine monks. St Benedict himself allowed for such a choice after long years of probation in community. Traces of Benedictine hermits, temporary or permanent, have been found in every century from the eighth to the eighteenth. Peter the Venerable had encouraged them in twelfth-century Cluny, so had the abbeys of St Albans and Westminster, both then and in the later Middle Ages, while the Durham series of hermits lasted almost to the Reformation. Whiterig's choice was not an isolated and extraordinary one, but one much more common in his day than in ours. Other examples have been recorded of Northern religious, especially Dominicans, choosing the eremitical life in the later Middle Ages, while at least seven hermits can be traced in the fourteenth century in the county of Durham, and seven more in Northumberland.[11]

When a person entered definitively on this form of life, a special consecration was made by the bishop together with the establishment of an enclosure in the case of an anchorite or an anchoress. Some texts of this ceremony, besides the constant teaching of spiritual writers, make it clear that the contemplative life must not be made an excuse for idleness. As in a monastery of cenobites the day was to be spent in a continual round of prayer, reading and manual work. The prayers prescribed were long, and hermits were expected to work at such tasks as gardening, bridge-building, road-mending and even lighthouse-keeping. Further, those capable of it were encouraged to write. Both Peter the Venerable and Guigo the Carthusian had recommended to solitaries the apostolate of the scribe, the latter in the memorable words that as the Carthusians 'could not preach with their lips, they should do so with their hands'.[12] Whiterig, in writing his meditations to be read by others, followed in the steps of many before him, among whom was Richard Rolle, while a few years after Whiterig's death Dame Julian of Norwich received and wrote of her 'shewings' of Christ's Passion. Such writing was regarded as a fitting occupation for those dedicated to a life of prayer and solitude.

IV. FARNE

Fifteen in number at high tide and twenty-eight at low tide, the Farne islands have changed very little since Whiterig's day. They are situated off the Northumbrian coast between Seahouses and Bamburgh, five miles south of Lindisfarne or Holy Island. There are two groups of them, divided by a wide and deep channel; they have no trees and few buildings, some of them have apparently never been inhabited by men, and all are now a unique bird sanctuary controlled by the National Trust. The grey-black rocks and sea which provide the dominant, sombre colour, the varied views of the mainland and the cry of the eider-ducks and other birds are all unchanged. The isolation is all but complete; if summer visitors enjoy unforgettable boat-trips there to see the seals and the very varied bird-life, few would venture to visit them, and still less to live on them in the depths of winter, when they are exposed to wind and storm and their austere beauty is all but hidden by low-lying mists which do not lift for days at a time.

The Inner Farne (called *Farneland* in the Durham documents) is both the largest of them all and the one nearest the coast, which is a mile and a half distant. On it are a restored medieval chapel and a tower built (or rebuilt) for defence purposes in *c.* 1500, the ruins of a second chapel parallel to the first, and of a guest-house near the jetty; at the other end of the island a lighthouse, now worked automatically, and two cottages built for its keepers but now uninhabited. These are situated on the cliffs at the south end of the island, and being painted white, are the island's most easily visible features.

The cliffs are approximately eighty feet high, and the land shelves down gradually to sea-level at the north end, where there is a tiny sand beach which provides the only possible place for a boat to land. All the ancient buildings and the water-supply are very close by. Traces remain of the monks' gardens, protected by walls from the wind and storms, where small crops were grown in the peaty soil which covers the rock. Now sea-campion grows over most of the island. Numerous inlets give the island variety in spite of its small extent, and the most interesting physical feature of all is the Churn, a fissure which extends from the sea inland near the north-west corner of the island. It is mostly bridged over with rock, but its innermost end is at an open shaft, and when a storm comes from the north the sea rushes up the channel, forces its way up the shaft and projects a column of water into the air, which sometimes reaches the height of ninety feet and can be seen from the mainland.[13]

Although only sixteen acres in extent at high tide, the Inner Farne is important in the history of the Church in England. Its first recorded inhabitant was St Aidan, the first bishop of Lindisfarne and apostle of Northumbria from 635 until his death on 31st August 651. Trained on the island monastery of Iona, and choosing Lindisfarne as his centre because of its re-semblance to it, Aidan, like other Celtic saints of his time, liked to retire to an even more remote island for solitude and prayer. The island he chose for this purpose was the Inner Farne, and it was from there that he saw and lamented the burning of Bamburgh by the heathen king Penda.[14]

It was St Cuthbert, however, who made Farne famous. This Northumbrian shepherd, who became a monk at Melrose under Aidan's disciple Eata and accepted with him the Roman Easter at the synod of Whitby, was appointed prior of Lindisfarne, where, by his gentle and persistent firmness in bringing the monks into line with the rest of the Catholic Church in their Easter observance and also perhaps by the introduction of the

Rule of St Benedict, he broke down opposition, and eventually won the hearts of all by his holiness, patience and charity. But in 676, seeking closer union with God through prayer and solitude, he retired to Farne after a preliminary trial of the eremitical life on the even smaller St Cuthbert's Isle, off Lindisfarne, which is within sight on a clear day of the Inner Farne, destined to be his home for the next eight years. Here he built himself a cell of unhewn stones and of turf, which was divided into two: one half being his oratory and the other his living-room. Most of the sites mentioned by the two contemporary lives can still be identified, although there are at least two opinions about that of his cell. The matter will only be finally settled, probably, by excavation. In 684 Cuthbert was compelled to leave his solitude for the cares of the bishopric of Lindisfarne, which extended through Northumberland as far west as Carlisle and Derwentwater, where his friend St Herbert also lived as a hermit. But after little more than two years as a bishop, Cuthbert, knowing his end was near, retired once more to Farne and died there on 20th March 687. Various natural features of the island are called by his name, such as St Cuthbert's Cove, St Cuthbert's Gut, etc., and even the eiders are still sometimes called St Cuthbert's ducks. The contemporary lives do not record his establishing a sanctuary for them, as was widely believed later in the Middle Ages, but they do describe his friendly contact with them, which seems to anticipate one of the most popular traits in the character of St Francis of Assisi.[15]

The example of St Cuthbert's life as a hermit on Farne inspired imitation. Aethilwald, Billfrith and Felgild succeeded him there, but in the subsequent anarchy of the Danish invasions there seems no certainty that Farne was again inhabited by hermits until the twelfth century. St Cuthbert, Northern England's most popular saint, still inspired monks of Durham to retire to the desert of Farne as he had done, and his incorrupt body, preserved after long wanderings through the North as Durham's most precious treasure, would have brought his example closer than any written records. Aelric, Aelwin and Thomas (formerly prior) are names of Durham monks who lived there in turn, but the most famous of them all was St Bartholomew of Farne, a Yorkshireman born at Whitby

and ordained prie$t in Norway who later became a monk at
Durham. When he entered the church to pray after receiving
the mona$tic habit, he saw in a vision the figure of Chri$t on the
Rood embrace him, and after a later vision of St Cuthbert
retired to Farne as a hermit, where he spent the remaining forty-
two years of his life from 1151 till 1193. A good contemporary
life of him by Geoffrey, monk of Coldingham, is $till extant
and was certainly known to John Whiterig (p. 88, note 447).[16]
Its description of Farne is well worth citing:

> Farne, which was formerly the fortress of devils, is now a cloi$ter
> and a school of saints. It is a kind of purgatory on earth, wisely
> e$tablished for the healing of both souls and bodies. It always
> contains, indeed it a&ually forms men of virtue, because when
> someone is led by the Spirit into its desert, he must expe& to be
> tempted by the devil. Consequently he either cultivates san&ity
> or else he leaves this holy place. And the $trength of temptation
> is greatly increased by the island's poverty and the cold caused by
> the sea.
>
> In shape it is almo$t round. A rocky eminence shelves down to
> a grassy level place, half of which, if cultivated, will yield a crop
> of barley, while the other half provides pa$ture for cattle. . . .
> There is a continual assault from the waves and ceaseless confli&
> with them: sometimes the island is completely covered with foam,
> which flows in from the sea and is blown over it by the wind, and
> this is a great mortification to those who live there, and it makes
> them cold and afraid. . . . Many islands are subje& to this one's
> dominion: one provides it with hay, another with fuel, while a
> third is a cemetery for (shipwrecked) sailors.
>
> Eider-ducks come there for ne$ting and are so tame that they
> do not mind human company. Although they love quiet, they are
> not di$turbed by noise. They make their ne$ts all round the
> island . . . . no one presumes to mole$t them or touch their eggs
> without leave, except the monks, who take a few for themselves
> and their gue$ts. . . . If the indu$trious ancients had known of
> Farne island's special privileges, they would have sung its praises
> throughout the world.

Another twelfth-century monk of Durham, Reginald, friend
of St Ailred of Rievaulx and biographer of St Godric of
Finchale, who in his sea-faring days used to visit Farne on pil-
grimage, also described the Farne eider-ducks as being so tame
since St Cuthbert's time that they ne$t in houses and allow

themselves to be touched, captured and held in one's hands. The chicks, whom Geoffrey describes as taking to the water as soon as they are hatched out, Reginald characterizes as ready to ſtay in the visitor's lap or under his clothes, while the ducks will come to table to receive food and make their neſts under his bed or in his blankets. If encouraged, they will follow the visitor round the island. There can be little doubt that medieval devotees of St Cuthbert would have warmly approved the reservation of the Farne islands as a sanctuary. To this day the eider-duck's peculiar cry, 'a plaintive long drawn note ending abruptly in a sharp barking noise' seems to sum up the atmosphere of Farne.[17]

In 1255 Durham eſtablished a regular cell on Farne. Two monks, removable by the prior, remained there almoſt continuously until the Reformation. The Farne records begin in 1357 and from them can be gleaned some details of the lives of the monks there. When Whiterig settled there, he would have lived the ordinary monaſtic routine of prayer, ſtudy and work in the auſtere and even grim environment which, as we have seen, resulted in the survival on Farne only of those who were spiritually the ſtrongeſt. The meditations themselves are evidence for Whiterig's prayer and ſtudy, and in one of them (p. 134) he mentions that his manual work included chopping wood, presumably washed ashore by the sea. Another ativity of the Farne monks was fishing. Their rather scanty endowments were supplemented by the sale of seal-oil, fish, eider-duck eggs and porpoises for feaſt-day fare at Durham. In 1365–6 they repaired their boat, fitting it with a new sail and four oars, and bought twelve fishing-lines and a net to use from it. Not content with this, they bought a new boat next year besides repairing the old one. Other expenses include the purchase of a mill, which suggeſts that some kind of grain was grown there. Curiously enough, there is no mention of liveſtock in the records of this date. The largeſt expense during Whiterig's ſtay on Farne was £22 5s. 6d. for the repair and alteration of the chapel during 1370–1. This would presumably have included the coſt of the windows on the south and eaſt walls of the chapel, in Decorated ſtyle like Fossor's windows at Durham. In the same year the ſtatues of St John and St Cuthbert in the same chapel were repainted at the coſt of 10s. 6d.

A reader of the meditations can hardly fail to be ſtruck by the large number of citations in them from other works. It may well be asked how the hermit had apparently such a large number of books available on his island home. The frequent quotations from St Auguſtine's *De Civitate Dei,* St Gregory's Homilies on the Gospels and St Bernard's Sermons on the Canticles sometimes by chapter would seem to indicate that at leaſt the relevant portions of these long works were either lent to him or else formed part of the Farne library. The same would be true of a copy of the whole Bible. It is also likely that he had his own commonplace book of citations from his previous *leĉtio divina* like other monks of the later Middle Ages. A Durham MS. now MS. Laud. Misc. 402 in the Bodleian Library at Oxford, contains among other items works by Hugh of St Viĉtor and Pecham's poem *Philomena,* both of which are cited in the Meditations, possibly from this very manuscript.[19]

The earlieſt inventory of the Farne books dates from 1394. The twelve volumes include a Book of the Sentences by Peter Lombard, a book of Decretals, a life of St Bartholomew of Farne, a book of meditations and prayers, a book of the Miracles of St Cuthbert, and a traĉt on the articles of faith, together with the miracles of our Lady and the Purgatory of St Patrick. There was also a Rule of St Auguſtine and two copies of the Office of the Dead. Apart from this the necessary liturgical books are not mentioned in the liſt because they were kept in the church. There were a few more whose contents cannot be identified, either because they are described in too general a way as, for inſtance, *liber continens xiii quaternos qui continent xiii traĉtatus,* or because they were in such bad condition that they are dismissed as other books whose 'outside tables are burnt by fire'. Meagre and incomplete as this information is, it does give some idea at leaſt of the number and kind of books accessible to a monk who lived as a hermit on Farne.

V. Meditations

Seven in number and of unequal length and quality, the Farne meditations form a coherent whole which reveals their author as one whose outlook was completely centred on the Person of Christ, and who, while being a sturdy traditionalist, was also sensitive to the more affective piety of his own day. His very choice of meditations as his literary form is significant. These had been popularized by writers of the eleventh century like St Anselm and John of Fécamp, and can be compared with more elaborate productions with many subdivisions favoured by St Edmund of Canterbury, John Mirk and others. Also typical of his deep roots in the past are his frequent use of texts from the Bible, the Fathers and the Liturgy, which are woven together with great skill in the style of St Bernard, who indeed was probably the greatest non-Scriptural influence on our author. His affinity with other writers of his age may be seen especially in his tender devotion to the Crucified Christ, which is nevertheless restrained, and far from the sentimentality of certain other writers of the later Middle Ages. These features, together with his emphasis on doctrine rather than on feeling, tend to give to his writing a timeless rather than a 'period' flavour, and should prove attractive to readers of our own day.

The first of the seven meditations, addressed to Christ Crucified, is nearly twice as long as all the others put together and is also the most important. A miniature treatise on the spiritual life, its principal theme is God's love for men, revealed especially by Christ's death on the Cross, which requires man's total love in return as the only attitude befitting a redeemed creature. This meditation is also the key to the others, which reveal the author's thought about our Lady, the Angels and his favourite saints, all of whom have already been mentioned at some length in that to Christ Crucified. It seems likely that this was written first.

This meditation falls naturally into three main parts. After an introductory chapter Christ is addressed under a series of Old Testament types including Adam, Abel, Noah, Isaac, Joseph, Samson and David (cc. 2–12).[19a] Here biblical citations abound, perhaps excessively. The most important chapter of the section (c. 11) presents God's Son speaking to the Father on our behalf and expressing his readiness to undergo the Incarnation in order to fight and conquer the devil, a patristic rather than an Anselmian presentation. Then follows the first of several verse passages, presumably by the author, which form an unusually interesting feature of these writings. They are translated below in the same metre and rhyming scheme as the original.

The second part of this meditation is a direct consideration of the crucified Christ from several different points of view. His various sufferings for our sake are listed with deep sympathy and reverence. In return Christ asks for man's heart and his love (cc. 16–17), and this return should be complete (cc. 18–19).

> I know well, Lord, that thou desirest my whole self when thou askest for my heart, and I seek thy whole self when I beg for thee. I know too, Lord, that thou wishest to possess me entirely in order that thou mayest be entirely possessed thyself, and this thou dost for my sake, not for thine own (p. 47).

The devout soul is visited by Christ with extraordinary sweetness and joy; such experiences gave surpassing strength to the martyrs and saints of old (cc. 20–21). These examples of the triumph of divine grace lead on to a brief consideration of predestination (c. 23) and the danger of blindness of heart and ingratitude (cc. 24–26), shown especially by lack of charity and preferring creatures to the Creator (cc. 27–29).

Nevertheless none should despair of God's mercy. The sacraments of Baptism and Penance were instituted to enable us to return to God. Christ has given us a sign of hope: that sign is himself, with arms extended on the cross to embrace man and draw him to union with himself. In comparison with knowing this sign of Christ Crucified, other knowledge is rather ignorance (cc. 30–39).

The meaning of the sign of Christ Crucified is then explained according to the allegorical, the moral and the anagogical senses (cc. 39–49). Allegorically the outstretched arms represent the Law and the Prophets or the two Testaments; morally we are led into the heart of Christ to be united with him who by a word created the universe, anagogically the right hand signifies eternity, the left hand riches and glory in this present world, through which the Church passes to enjoy the embrace of her bridegroom in heaven.

Then the author exhorts the reader to draw near in spite of his unworthiness and learn to read the open book of the Saviour's body on the cross (cc. 51–52). The letters of this book are his wounds; the words are his actions and sufferings (c. 53). Knowledge of this book is necessary for salvation, a deep knowledge of assimilation obtained by metaphorical eating and digesting, which will lead us by penance to complete what is lacking in the sufferings of Christ.

In the two following chapters occur the culminating points of this section of the meditation. The author sees the events of his past life as the expression of God's merciful love on his behalf:

> Thou, sweet Jesus, art all my good: thou art my ability in work and eloquence in conversation, my proficiency in study and achievement in enterprise, my consolation in adversity and caution in prosperity. Whichever way I turn, thy grace and mercy go before me, and often when it seemed that all was over with me, thou didst suddenly deliver me. Thou didst bring me back when I went astray and instruct me in my ignorance; thou didst correct me in my sin, console me in my sorrow and comfort me in my despair. . . . (p. 78).

During a crisis caused by this despair, the author experienced a vision of Christ himself, who consoled him.

> O Lord of hosts, Jesus most lovable, what caused thee to be so solicitous in my regard that thou hast not only willed that the heart of thy servant should experience that delightful, hidden presence, which overflows with fullness of joy and avails for love's close embraces, not only chosen to give me that hope which thou givest to other sons of the Church through patience and the consolation of the Scriptures; that would not suffice thee, but over and above it all thou must needs teach me, not through thy beloved evangelist John who proffered my petition to thee, but with thine own mouth, how I could be saved on the day of Judgement; for that was my petition. Merrily and with mild countenance thou didst call out in reply: 'Love, and thou shalt be saved' (ibid.).

This section concludes with a prayer of confidence, that as Christ has given this pledge to the writer, so he will deign to lead him further towards the heights:

'Perfect, good Jesus, what thou hast wrought in me . . . . what I ask for is exceedingly great and sublime, and can only be reached by degrees' (c. 58).

This mention of the degrees of love leads on to the third part of the meditation (cc. 59–98), which is a short treatise on the spiritual life, seen as the progressive ascending of these various degrees by the faithful and grateful soul. Although the author nowhere says: 'Love is repaid by love alone', this saying of the best known modern saint does sum up the thought of the monk of Farne.[20] And like St Bernard, whose influence in this section is both obvious and dominant, Whiterig saw the development of the spiritual life in terms of the progress of charity. 'St Bernard', wrote one of his modern disciples, 'wrote no treatise on mysticism; for him mysticism is quite simply the last rung on the ladder of charity. . . . St Bernard's mysticism is not in function of mental prayer, it is simply a perfect participation in the love which God has for himself: *sic affici deificari est*'.[21] The monk of Farne cited and made his own many of the fundamental texts of St Bernard's mystical teaching, and the same principles of interpretation should be applied to each. Here it may be remarked that nowhere does the monk of Farne posit a division of the spiritual life into two sections, 'ordinary', and 'extraordinary' or 'mystical', but clearly sees the unfolding of the life of grace and charity as one single process with the highest degree of charity (including mystical experience) at the end. Of his own experience he says little beyond the passage from c. 55 already cited: but he envisaged the highest degree of charity as something within range of his practical aspirations as well as of his speculative thought.

The progress of the soul towards God is traced through the early stages of what St Bernard called carnal love of Christ by means of hearing of Christ and mortification (cc. 60–62). Then are described the stages of a more rational love: study of Christ, joy and unworldliness reached through trying always to do what pleases Christ, whatever the consequences and in all circumstances (cc. 63–72). To these stages correspond the precept to love God *toto corde* and *tota anima*; to love *tota virtute* corresponds a third stage of unitive love, characterized by extreme ardour combined with liberty, by distaste for the present life and finally by a certain loss of the uses of the senses and even by death through charity rather than through any particular disease. This phenomenon was also described by St John of the Cross.[22]

As he could not describe such events from his experience

Whiterig made use of the witness of other writers. First of all, he cites the relevant stanzas of the long lyrical poem *Philomena* by archbishop Pecham, which describes the death of the nightingale as a figure of the death of a spiritual person from the love of God (cc. 83–84). Another example is given in a delightful story of a medieval solitary, told in a revelation that a certain girl in a distant province was predestined to the same degree of glory as himself. When he went to visit her, he found that she appeared to do nothing extraordinary either in her devotions or in her austerities, but that she was a virgin who had dedicated herself to the love of God in great and continual joy. During the hermit's visit she died from no other apparent cause (c. 85). Further descriptions of this highest degree of divine love are cited from standard authors, especially Hugh of St Victor. Our Lady and St John are evoked as examples of saints who were spared the martyrdom of the sword so that they could die as martyrs of divine love (cc. 94–95). The author then expresses the wish that he might be guided in the spiritual life by one who experienced its highest degrees (c. 97), and sees in the lives of such souls the vindication of the Incarnation and Passion of Christ.

> I know, Lord, and I know it well and truly, that from all eternity thou didst foresee such as would be wounded by the darts of thy love, and so thou didst take flesh. To redeem them thou didst choose to die, not that they had merited thine incarnation and death, as though anyone had first given to thee and afterwards thou hadst repaid him, but it was rather by virtue of thy death that they were able to do what thou didst from all eternity foresee they would do. Thus thy death .... was itself the cause and origin of every meritorious act whatsoever (p. 110).

This meditation then ends with a prayer in prose and verse for present needs and final perseverance.

After this summary of the longest meditation, some characteristic features may be underlined. The author's personal devotion to Christ and his frequent representation of the wisdom of the past as expressed in Scripture, the Liturgy and the Fathers have already been noted. He relies on the soundest teachers rather than on his own experience, and this is not surprising in view of his comparatively limited knowledge. His doctrinal emphasis and his disciplined restraint, together with his taste for traditional spiritual wisdom, are almost certainly charateristic of the monastery which formed him.

We may also note his special prayer for the Durham community to which he still belonged (pp. 110, 153), and it is perhaps significant that there is no specifically eremitical tendency expressed in his writings. Nor is there even a description of his own surroundings or a passage in praise of solitude. Of his abandonment of the amenities of Durham for the bleak austerity of Farne he tells us nothing, and only as *obiter dicta* does he let fall a few scraps of information about his former life, such as his escape from death at the age of eight (p. 134). Like many other monks before and since, he was more concerned with Christ than with spiritual autobiography, with sound doctrine than the description of his experiences.

In contrast to the author of the *Cloud of Unknowing*, he shows no trace of the negative or so-called Dionysian approach to contemplation: his experience of prayer seems to have been through the formulae of the Liturgy, fed by assiduous meditation on Holy Scripture. In contrast to Margery Kempe and even to Methley there seems to have been nothing unbalanced or overwrought about him. In contrast to Rolle, he considered the Passion not in terms of the bursting out from Christ's limbs of the Precious Blood, but insead he compared the honour shown to the sacred Head by angels with the insults and sufferings inflicted on it by men on Calvary. Here he was perhaps nearer to both St Thomas and St Bonaventure than to some of his contemporaries, but the Cistercian Rymington wrote at least one passage on the Passion very similar to Whiterig's.[22a]

But by his treatment of the Sacred Heart the author deserves a small place among the spiritual writers from St Gertrude to St Margaret Mary Alacoque who propagated this devotion. Whiterig wrote of the Sacred Heart as of a refuge of sinners:

Precisely because I am a sinner, I have fled to thee, since there is nowhere I can flee from thee save to thee....I will run to my Lord as he beckons me to come, and by touching him I shall be cleaned from all impurity of body and soul....I will enter into thee and not stay without, for outside thee there is no salvation....Kind, humble heart, allow me to hide with thee from the face of the Lord's anger, for he is coming to judge the world. If thou choosest the left side, then let me remain on the right: Christ's body is not so strait that it cannot hold us both at once. So let us make here two tabernacles, one for thee and one for me, and there will still be room for Abraham, Isaac and Jacob to take their places, together with all those who follow their way of life. And the heart of Jesus answers me: 'If thou didst not desire to dwell with me, I would not have allowed thee to enter here. But now, since it is my delight to dwell with the sons of men, I will not cast out him that cometh to me. Where I am, there let him be whom I love and by whom I am loved.'

Whiterig gives the impression of a sane, holy and well-adjusted person. One point which illustrates this is his admirable balance between compunction and joy. He had neither the gloom of the Puritan nor the superficial neglect of repentance. Other passages already cited are sufficient evidence for his compunction; the following shows his thought on joy:

Cheerfulness adds just as much to our actions as action adds to a right intention, for cheerfulness in the doer is at once both a sign and an effect of a loving heart, and if we have not got that, all that we do goes awry (c. 68).

Lastly, it may be asked whether the monk of Farne was anti-intellectual: in some passages he attacks those who prefer knowledge to piety, in others he exalts the kind of knowledge which cannot come from books (c. 63). But parallels to these passages can be found in the Fathers, and even St Thomas Aquinas praised the old woman who knew more about the immortality of the soul than the philosophers.[23] In fact the theme is almost perennial, and can be traced back to St Paul's teaching on the wisdom of this world contrasted with that of Christ crucified. St Bernard too had written in similar vein, and here too it is helpful to study St Bernard's thought if we are to understand Whiterig: each was representative of monastic spirituality on the relation between learning and charity.

Both would have agreed that reading and meditation, especially of Holy Scripture, are a preparation for contemplation;

if they are to be fruitful, continual effort at penetration and memorizing must be made. But in moments of contemplation all images are suspended, and the soul adheres to the Mystery of God without being able to explain it. Hence St Gregory's saying, cited by Whiterig, that love is itself a kind of knowledge, and Ambrose Autpert's teaching: 'If we seek to understand thee, we do not discover thee as thou art; it is by love alone that thou art attained.' William of St Thierry among others, taught the same.[24]

In doing so, he and others were representative of monastic spiritual writers, who combined a just appreciation of the primacy of charity in contemplation with a proportionate emphasis on the importance of the preparatory intellectual element of *lectio divina*. St Bernard did not want his monks to be foolish,[25] and every page of the Farne meditations is witness to our author's assiduity in sacred reading. Neither would have supported a cult of ignorance or encouraged the suppression of intellectual activity in spiritual matters, but both recommended the *simplification* of intellectual activity in harmony with an asceticism which should lead to perfect union of God by charity. Nevertheless meditation on the truths of faith through *lectio divina* is its normally indispensable preliminary.

The meditations to the saints share the same general outlook as that to Christ Crucified, of which indeed they may be considered the completion. In that work warnings were given against the undue exaltation of any creature (cc. 27–28), culminating in these words:

'Therefore do not by your love make for yourself a god of any one save him alone who loved us so greatly when we did not as yet exist. I do not forbid the love of the saints, but I do desire that right order should be kept in loving them' (p. 56).

This admirable recommendation was kept by the author no doubt, but there is one passage in the meditation to our Lady which seems to contradict it. Misled by a text attributed to St Augustine, the author, whose intentions were perfectly orthodox, fell into some well-meant inaccuracy of language. Taken out of its context the sentence 'The flesh of Mary is God and may be adored without blame' could be condemned as heretical.

But when we look into the context of such an astonishing statement we find that the phrase 'the flesh of Mary' is used of the humanity of Christ, not of the flesh of Mary's own body. It means, as the author says, 'the flesh which thou dost possess in thy Son, for it will never cease to be thine own flesh since he will never cease to be thine own son' (p. 123). Such an explanation exonerates him from any evil or erroneous intention, but his choice of language was, to say the least, unfortunate. In the same meditation he described the sanctification of Mary at the Annunciation by the Holy Spirit as including the elimination of 'every trace of original sin in thee'. At the time when the author wrote this, the Immaculate Conception was not a dogma, but a matter of theological opinion. Scotists insisted on the unique privileges accorded to the Mother of God, while Thomists insisted rather on the need of every creature, Mary included, for the grace of Redemption, accomplished through the death of her Son on the cross. Each side had one aspect of the truth, and what was good in each was included in the definitive settlement of the controversy by the Bull *Ineffabilis Deus* of Pius IX in 1854.

The author's Mariology is not the only example of Thomist influence upon him. Others are his statements about the infusion of individual souls into bodies which are already *organizata*, the non-composite nature of the angels and the lack of temporal priority in the stages of Creation. But Thomist influence may well have been much more extensive: in the Durham library there are still to be found eighteen out of the twenty-three medieval manuscripts of St Thomas' works formerly there; among the survivors are two exceptionally early ones.

On the subject of the angels the author's personal affective outlook is again very much in evidence, and his meditation forms a notable addition to the series of medieval prayers to the angels collected by Dom Wilmart.[26] It is also closely connected with an English prayer to the Guardian Angel preserved in another Durham manuscript book of meditations (A, IX, 24):

> Myn angel that art to me ysend
>   Fro God to be my Governour,
> Fro all yvyl thu me defend
>   In every dyssese be my succour.

This meditation, which contains most of his autobiographical data, is also one in which the author recalls the theological teaching he had received years ago, and shows sufficient interest in disputed points to opt for the opinion of Peter the Lombard and St Thomas on the angels' spirituality and for that of St Gregory and St Bernard on the role of the Seraphim and other higher angels.

The meditation on David and Abraham is more unusual in its subject-matter and is written evidence for medieval devotion to the patriarchs and prophets so often shown in sculpture, stained glass and miniature painting. In the early chapters of the meditation to Christ Crucified the patriarchs were seen as types of Christ and David as a type of the Church, but now they are studied rather as models respectively of obedience and repentance. Both are invoked in face of the 'misery and pestilence by which we are afflicted'. Also worthy of note is the author's supposition that Adam had lived for only six hours before the Fall, an opinion much nearer St Irenaeus' 'child Adam' than St Thomas' picture of a perfect adult man. On a less serious level we may also notice, apropos of a jocular use of words of the Psalter in an accommodated sense:

'Any comedian, out to raise a laugh in his audience, would find passages from the psalms, did he but know them and care to make use of them, which would enhance his performance; though to debase such sacred mystic words to such profanities would be no slight sin' (c. 9).

Only one of the two meditations to St John the Evangelist has been printed in this volume. The second and longer one contains developments on the subject of the 'manna' reported by the Golden Legend and earlier writings to flow from his tomb. This phenomenon, also found by St Benedict's tomb at Monte Cassino, is probably due to an emanation of saltpetre or some other chemical substance of purely natural origin. Also in this meditation is found an opinion based on St Peter Damian's sermons 63 and 64, that St John, like the Blessed Virgin, enjoyed the privilege of corporal assumption into Heaven. Such a speculation, unsupported by Scriptural, conciliar or patristic texts is as unlikely as the supposition, put forward by certain theologians in our own day, of an Immaculate Conception of St Joseph.

The final meditation to St Cuthbert is unfortunately incom‐
plete. It might have told us more both about Durham and about
hermit life on Farne in the footSteps of St Cuthbert. But it is
perhaps moSt reasonable to suppose that death overtook John
Whiterig before he could complete it, that, worn out by the
auSterity of the Farne hermitage or attacked by the plague, he
passed while Still relatively young to that perfeCt love of God
whose earlier Stages he had already described in the meditation
to ChriSt Crucified.

For the contemporary reader the timeless elements of the Farne
meditations will appeal, even if the mode of expression is occa‐
sionally unfamiliar. The cult of ChriSt crucified and devotion
to the saints who modelled their lives on his are as necessary
and desirable today as in the fourteenth century. The degrees
of the love of God have not changed since then, nor are the
sacrifices necessary to attain its heights any the less taxing; the
exigencies of the Gospel do not change from one age to another.
His Strongly Scriptural outlook will appeal to the present age of
revived intereSt in Biblical Studies, his writings will throw light
on the mentality of the late medieval cloiStered monk, while his
personal religion, expressed in the extraCts printed below as well
as in those already cited, should prove attraCtive to many.

Give me thyself, and the reSt take for thyself.... Whatever there is
besides thee does not satisfy me without thee, nor haSt thou any gift
to beStow which I desire so much as thee (c. 5).

I see thee, good Jesus, nailed to the Cross, crowned with thorns,
given gall to drink, pierced with the lance and for my sake dislocated
in all thy limbs on the gibbet of the Cross. How greatly thou haSt
loved me since, whereas thou art thyself moSt good, for me thou
haSt desired to be reckoned among the wicked; being thyself moSt
beautiful, for me thou haSt desired to be accounted a leper and the
laSt of men; being thyself Strong and powerful, for me thou didSt
allow thyself to be executed like a thief; being thyself wise, for me
thou didSt desire to be the butt of mocking words and geStures from
those who Stood round the Cross, and so all that was within or
without thee caused thee suffering for my sake (c. 13).

From all this one can gather how much God should be loved by man, since he has deigned to suffer so much for him. In return for all this he asks nothing but that man should love him above all things (c. 14).

Remember, sweet Jesus, whom I seek to please, that it is Thee I desire to love above all. Make me joyfully to fulfil thy commands so that I may see thy face for ever, and deal with me so mercifully before I die that I may know that I love nothing so much as God. May I be protected by thy hand from all present evils, and find firm support in the sign of victory! Ward off famine, foe and plague, grant us all-pervading peace, and for the sake of tranquillity cause brethren to be of one mind. Put an end to wars, keep far from us the deadly injury of sin; and lest souls rush headlong to perdition, be thou to us a tower of strength! (c. 98).

Notes to Introduction

1. Cf. W. A. Pantin, 'Two Treatises of Uthred of Boldon on the Monastic Life' in *Studies ... presented to F. M. Powike* (Oxford 1953), 363–385.
2. A sentence is left unfinished on f. 8r. After *exibicio* (f. 15v) *vel apposicio* is interlined. Other mistakes include *denec* for *donec* (f. 18v), *quin* for *quam* (f. 20v), *volumina* for *molimina* (f. 22v), *antende* for *attende* (f. 24v), *sucut* for *sicut* (f. 39v), *ubi* for *nisi* (f. 41v), *contites* for *contines* (f. 51v), *vetide* for *vetite* (f. 61r), *pro ve* for *prout* (f. 72v), *veritute* for *veritate* (f. 72v).
3. Farne Rolls 1371; Durham Bursar's Rolls 1371.
4. Hatfield's Register, 65–7; P.H. Reaney, A Dictionary of English Surnames (London 1958), 352.
5. *Register of Richard of Bury* (SS 1910), 154–5. Seventy-three Durham monks took part in Hatfield's election in 1345. Cf. Cart. Misc. 2636.
6. Cf. M. Mackisack, *The Fourteenth Century* (Oxford 1959), 115–9, W. A. Pantin, *Chapters of the English Black Monks* (*CS*), iii, 200–201.
7. *Rites of Durham* (ed. J. T. Fowler, SS 1902), 18.
8. Cf. W. A. Pantin, *The English Church in the Fourteenth Century* (Cambridge 1955).
8a. For Uthred of Boldon cf. W. A. Pantin, *The English Church in the Fourteenth Century* (Cambridge 1955), 165–75; M. D. Knowles, *The Religious Orders in England* (Cambridge 1955), ii, 48–54, 61–89; 'The Censured Propositions of Uthred of Boldon' in *British Academy Proceedings* xxxvii, 1952, 305–42; D. H. Farmer, The 'Meditacio Devota' of Uthred of Boldon in *Analecta Monastica*, V (Rome 1958), 187–206.
9. Cf. M. D. Knowles, *op. cit.* 39–61, 362–3; D. H. Farmer (ed.), *Benedict's Disciples* (2nd ed. Gracewing 1994)
9a. *Ecclesiae Dunelmensis Scriptores Tres* (SS 1839), 130–7.
10. *Ibid.* 137–42; *Bishop Hatfield's Survey* (SS 1856) iv–vii. Hatfield's visitation of 1354 produced a crop of accusations against the prior and several obedientiaries. These were largely unfounded, and Hatfield's final injunctions

show that the administration and discipline at Durham were at a high level. There should be more consultation about administration, a resident doctor should be provided as before, and there are injunctions about the sick, recreations and almsgiving. Cf. B. Harbottle, 'Bishop Hatfield's Visitation of Durham Priory in 1354', *Archaeologia Aeliana*, XXXVI (1958), 81–100.

11. Cf. R. M. Clay, *The Hermits and Anchorites of England* (London 1914), especially Appendix C, and the same author's 'Further Studies on Medieval Recluses', *JBAA*, 1953, 74–86, and 'Some Northern Anchorites' in *Archaeologia Aeliana*, XXXIII (1955), 202–17. See also M. D. Knowles, *op. cit.*, II, 219–22; and J. Leclercq, 'Pierre le Vénérable et l'Erémetisme Clunisien in *Petrus Venerabilis, Studia Anselmiana*, 44 (Rome 1956), 99–120.

12. Guigonis *Consuetudines, PL* 153, 694.

13. For the Farne islands see T. R. Goddard and G. Hickling, *Guide to the Farne Islands* (Newcastle 1959); A. Watkin, 'Farne Island and St Cuthbert' in *Downside Review*, 1952, 292–307; C. Eyre, *The History of St Cuthbert*, (London 1887) 32–85.

14. Bede, *Historia Ecclesiastica gentis Anglorum*, III, 16 (ed. C. Plummer, (Oxford 1896), i, 158–9).

15. For St Cuthbert cf. *Two Lives of St Cuthbert* (ed. B. Colgrave) (Cambridge 1940), especially pp. 95–107, 129–31, 267–89. St Cuthbert's cell, usually believed to be under the present tower, where there is a spring of fresh water, was believed by Archbishop Eyre, followed by Dom A. Watkin, to have been on another site, which formerly contained a second spring, now dried up.

16. Symeon of Durham, *Opera* (*R. S.*), i, 295–325.

17. Reginald of Durham, *De admirandis virtutibus B. Cuthberti* (*SS* 1835), 60–3. See also pp. 71–9, 131–9, 300, etc., for further descriptions of Farne and its inhabitants. Another twelfth-century collection of these stories was edited by Sir E. Craster, 'The Miracles of St Cuthbert at Farne' in *Analecta Bollandiana*, LXX (1952), 5–19; translation in *Archaeologia Aeliana*, XXIX (1951) 93–107. A. Watkin, *art. cit.* 306.

18. Extracts from the Farne accounts and inventories were printed by J. Raine, *North Durham*, 345–59.

19. For other examples of monks' commonplace books cf. W. A. Pantin, 'English Monks before the Suppression of the Monasteries' in *Dublin Review*, 1937, 250–70.

19a. Cf. H. de Lubac, Exégèse Mediévale (Paris 1959), 445. Much of this section reproduces traditional patristic allegory.

20. Cf. Thérèse of Lisieux, *Autobiography of a Saint* (tr. R. A. Knox), 236.

21. Cf. A. le Bail, article 'Bernard' in *Dictionnaire de Spiritualité*, II, 1478–82.

22. Cf. St John of the Cross, *Complete Works* (tr. E. A. Peers), iii, 32.

22a. For Rymington, monk of Salley, who became Chancellor of Oxford University in 1372 cf. F. J. E. Raby, *Poems of John of Hoveden* (*SS* 1939), xxxvi–vii, and J. McNulty, 'William of Rymington, Prior of Salley Abbey' in *Yorks Archaeological Journal*, XXX, 1931, 231–47. For the English Mystics in general, cf. D. Knowles, *The English Mystical Tradition*; for Margery Kempe, W. Butler-Bowden, *The Book of Margery Kempe*; for Methley, D. Knowles, *The Religious Orders in England*, II, 224–6; for Rolle, his *English Writings* (ed. H. E. Allen), especially 36 and his *Minor Works* (ed. P. Hodgson), especially 161.

23. Cf. St Thomas Aquinas, *Opera* (ed. Fiette), vol. XXII, 676; à Kempis, *Imitation of Christ*, i, 3.

24. Cf. J. Leclercq and J-M. Dechanet, article 'Contemplation' in *Dictionnaire de Spiritualité*, II, 1946–1965; E. Gilson, *Mystical Theology of St Bernard*, Appendix V, 95.

25. St Bernard, *Sermo* 69 in *Cantica Canticorum*, PL 183, 1113.

26. A. Wilmart, *Auteurs Spirituels et Textes Devotes du Moyen-Age*, 537–58.

THE MEDITATIONS OF A CERTAIN MONK

Sometime hermit on Farne Island

Meditation addressed to Christ crucified

I WILL speak to my Lord, though I be but dust and ashes,[1] and I beseech thee, Lord, be not angry if I speak this once, though a man of polluted lips,[2] unworthy to proclaim thy justice or to take thy covenant in my mouth, since I have rejected thy discipline, turning instead to vain sayings, and have cast thy words behind me.[3] Cleanse then, good Lord, the iniquity of my lips,[4] and with thy discipline correct me unto the end[5]; open thou my mouth, and give me a right and well-sounding speech in thy presence today, for there is no confusion to them that trust in thee, O Lord.[6]

Though I have sinned and done evil before thee,[7] and so provoked thee to wrath, yet it is when I am aware of thy anger that I have the greatest confidence in thy clemency,[8] for when thou hast been angry, thou wilt show mercy.[9] God is my witness that I speak peace concerning thee, not in order to search into thy majesty (in such peace were indeed bitterness most bitter,[10] for it would be very bitter to me to be overwhelmed by thy glory), but in order to declare unto my brethren thy name[11] and how good it is in the sight of thy servants, because thou hast delivered the poor from the mighty, the poor man who had no helper.[12] Thou hast spared the poor and the needy, judged for the orphan and the humble, and saved the souls of the poor.[13] Thou hast turned our mourning into joy[13a] by humbling the calumniator, of whom it is written: 'My people went down into Egypt to sojourn there, and Assur hath oppressed them without any cause'.[14] Assur, which is interpreted 'merchant' or 'rich man',[15] may well signify the devil, prince of this world, whose eyes behold all that is lofty, and who is himself king of all the sons of pride who go down to the sea in ships, trafficking in the great waters.[16] Thou hast put down this mighty one from the throne which he strove to erect towards the north, and hast exalted the humble,[17] raising up the needy, and lifting up the poor from the dunghill to sit with princes[18] and hold the throne of glory, from which the accuser of our brethren has been cast down.[19] For this it is indeed meet and juſt that the poor and needy should praise thy name,[20] seeing that thou haſt made their name honourable in thy sight.[21]

(Ch. 2).   Thou art Adam: not indeed the firſt Adam, who complied with the woman's suggeſtion, but the second, whom a virgin conceived, remaining after childbirth a virgin.[22] Thou art Abel, whose offerings were acceptable in the sight of the Lord, who required not indeed a burnt-offering for sin, but was appeased when thou didſt say: 'Behold I come'.[23] Thou art Noe, which means 'reſting',[24] and which I can well underſtand applies to thee, either because on the seventh day in the beginning, having made heaven and earth and all things that are under the vault of heaven,[25] thou didſt reſt from all the work which thou hadſt done,[26] or because thou haſt given us reſt from our enemies and from the hand of all who hated us.[27] Thou haſt begotten three sons, the firſt without the covenant of circumcision, the second under it, the third in the order of grace, as it were Sem, Cham and Japhet.[28] For Sem means 'one who hears',[29] and is fittingly applied to the gentiles of whom the apoſtle asks: 'Have they not heard?'[30] They did indeed hear the Lord God speaking to them through the law written in their hearts, and saying: 'Do to others as you would be done by.'[31] Cham means 'warm',[32] and well describes the Jews, who were indeed warm towards God as far as legal ceremonies went, but were by no means on fire, because the law brought no one to perfeótion.[32a] But Japhet, the younger being frequently adorned with grace, is interpreted as 'breadth' or 'expansion',[33] and very aptly denotes us Chriſtians; this breadth or charity, which is God's commandment exceeding wide,[34] is poured abroad in our hearts by the Holy Spirit who is given to us,[35] in whom we cry: 'Abba, Father',[36] and who, by enlarging our hearts, has taught us to run the way of his commandments.[37] Thou, O Lord, doſt guide thy Church out of the ſtorms of this world far more securely than Noe kept the ark from the waters of the deluge.

Thou art Isaac, who didſt make laughter for us[38] by offering thyself to God in sacrifice upon a mount called Calvary. Thou art the ram, caught by the horns amidſt the briers, and sacrificed in place of the son[39]; for that which thou hadſt assumed succumbed to death, but thou who didst assume it couldst not succumb. And yet thou art not two but one; according to thy human nature thou didst die and wast buried, according to thy divinity thou didst remain unhurt. And thus, O good Jesus, thou didst make laughter for us amidst tears and music for us in thine own lament.

(Ch. 3). Thou art Jacob the supplanter, who hast supplanted them that rose up against us, and hast made our enemies turn their backs upon us; thou hast beguiled the devil, through whose envy death entered into the world; and this thou didst do so wisely and fittingly, that life rose up from thence whence death had sprung, and he, who by a tree had gained his victory, was likewise by a tree overcome.[40] Thou art the Good Shepherd who knowest thy sheep, and thine know thee, nor can anyone snatch them out of thy hand.[41] For we were once like sheep going astray, but thou didst come to seek us, and didst carry us on thy shoulders back to the flock, and so we were converted to the shepherd and bishop of our souls.[42] On this account must we perforce say to thee, as Isaac did to Jacob his son: 'Cursed be he that curseth thee; and let him that blesseth thee be filled with blessings. Let peoples serve thee and tribes worship thee; be thou lord of thy brethren, and let thy mother's children bow down before thee'[43]— the sons, that is, of the synagogue (most certainly not of the Virgin Mary), who at one time fought against thee, but for whom thou didst pray: 'Father forgive them for they know not what they do'.[44] For if they had known, they would never have crucified the Lord of glory.[45]

Thou shalt no longer be called Jacob, Lord, but Joseph shall be thy name,[46] which is interpreted 'increase' or 'joining'[47]. Either meaning is most fitting, because thou hast increased thy people exceedingly, and thou wast thyself joined to us, when the Word was made flesh and dwelt among us,[48] so that man could in very truth say unto thee: 'This is now bone of my bone and flesh of my flesh.'[49] With such increase did God increase us, that it is the same person whom the Father begot from all eternity and the Virgin brought forth in time.[50] It was this that the patriarchs awaited, this the prophets foretold, and all whom the Holy Spirit touched desired to see it. Assuredly a fair sight, worthy of all beholding, to see as man, not only the Creator of man, but the Maker of heaven and earth, of all things, visible and invisible.[51]

(Ch. 4). Thy mother made for thee a long tunic when thou didst take flesh from the Virgin. For thy tunic is thy humanity, which thy brethren the Jews crucified, hanging it upon the wood of the cross, that thy Father might see whether it were the tunic of his Son or not.[52] And thy Father, although he could not be deceived, could say with truth: 'An evil wild beast—the envy of the Jews—hath devoured my son Joseph.'[53] But thou, O Lord, before they struck and wounded thee, took thy garments, and cast lots for thy tunic,[54] didst come down into Egypt, and God was with thee; into a region that is of unlikeness, a land of misery and darkness.[55] Thou didst visit Hell, and to those who were in the pains of darkness didst give light to see thee. Thou broughtest forth the captives from the pit in which there is no water, and didst place them in a Paradise of pleasure, not to tend and keep it,[56] but to rest for the future from their labours.[57] Then thou wast taken up into the house of the King, not only of Egypt, but the King whose is the world and the fullness thereof,[58] the King of all kings and Lord of lords;[59] his kingdom is the kingdom of all ages,[60] and he has given thee all power in heaven and on earth.[61]

Remember us then, O Lord, when it shall be well with thee,[62] for thou art our brother and our flesh[63]; suggest to the Father that he should fill the sacks of thy brethren[64]— fill them, I mean, with that wheat which, once it had fallen into the ground and died,[65] brought forth much fruit, and filled every living creature with blessing.[66] Thou who knowest no ill-will towards thy brethren, grant us our measure of wheat. For we have no other advocate who has been made unto us justice and sanctification,[67] and whom the Father always hears for his reverence, but thee, good Lord, who art the propitiation for our sins.[68] Remember then, O Lord, when thou standest in the sight of God, to speak well on our behalf.[69] Ask thy Father to give me that wheat which with desire I have desired to eat before I die.[70]

(Ch. 5). I wish for no other wheat but thee: give me thyself, and the rest take for thyself.[71] For what have I in heaven, and what have I desired more than thee on earth?[72] Whatever there is besides thee does not satisfy me without thee, nor hast thou any gift to bestow which I desire so much as thee. If therefore thou hast a mind to satisfy my desire with good things, give me naught else but thyself. For my desire would not be pleasing in thy sight, if I longed for something other than thee more than for thee. I know that thou art a jealous lover, greatly yearning to be yearned for and loving to be loved, and there is no sin in the world for which thou art so wrath with man, as when thou seest that thou are not loved by him. O good Joseph, be mindful of me, Benjamin, because I am the youngest amongst my brethren, unworthy to be called 'son of the right hand' or of strength, but 'son of bitterness' is my name, because if I should think upon the days of old and have in mind the eternal years, I would recount them all to thee in the bitterness of my soul.[73]

(Ch. 6). Thou art that most meek man Moses, so named by the king's daughter because she drew him from the water; who when he was grown up slew the Egyptian, and forthwith buried him in the sand, lest he should be discovered, and who received the Law from the Lord on Mount Sinai, and led the sons of Jacob and Joseph out of Egypt. His grave or remains are known to no man, but he is said to have been buried by the Lord alone. The king's daughter is Mary, the water the Holy Spirit, through whose overshadowing the Virgin divinely conceived Christ, who by his cross and death overcame the devil and thrust him down to Hell for ever, as it were burying him in the sand.

> Who did save us, his law gave us: God's own house denotes the mount;
> Law he brought us which he taught us, we are saved on its account.

He led the sons of Jacob and Joseph out of Egypt when he saved us and redeemed us from the tyranny of Satan. No man beholds his tomb, in so far as that his body will not be shown to us before the day of judgement. This is no slight upon the Eucharist, for there it is a matter of faith not of vision. He is said to have been buried by the Lord alone, because his divinity but not his soul was with his body during the three days.

Thou art the brazen serpent hung upon the gibbet, a remedy to all believers against the bites of the devil.[74] Thou art the lonely sparrow upon a house-top,[75] and thou hast found a nest for thyself which is the Virgin's womb. Thou art the scapegoat, and hast carried our sins into the wilderness of eternal oblivion, so that as far as the east is from the west, so far should our iniquities be from us.[76] Thou art the lamb of God who takest away the sins of the world,[77] whom the assembly of the sons of Israel sacrificed, and whose flesh roasted at the fire we eat with wild lettuce,[78] as often as with burning love we receive the body of Christ in memory of his bitter passion.

(Ch. 7). O Lord and Father, how sweet is thy Spirit within us! In order to show thy loving kindness towards sinners,[79] thou didst not spare thine only-begotten Son[80] but in the inestimable love of thy charity didst deliver up the Son to redeem the servant![81] O ineffable obedience of the Son, who though Lord of all, splendour of the Father's glory and figure of his substance,[82] was condemned on behalf of his enemies to a most shameful death because he wished it,[83] and himself bore our sins,[84] thus paying the debt which he had not incurred, and taking up what he had not laid down![85] And he who had committed no sin, nor was guile found in his mouth,[86] was made sin for us in an odour of sweetness unto the Father.[87] This it is, O Lord, which above all else renders thee lovable to me, namely the chalice which thou hast drunk, the work of our Redemption.

There is amongst all the benefits which thou hast conferred upon the human race from the beginning none which claims my love with better right, none which affects me more powerfully, carrying me wholly as it does out of my very self, than that when we were thine enemies, thou didst reconcile us to God in thy blood, and through thy death didst make friends of thine enemies.[88] What heart, though it were of stone, would not melt to hear how the only-begotten Son of God was made obedient to the Father unto death, even unto the death of the cross,[89] which in those days was the most shameful? Verily if anyone on hearing this does not love the Lord Jesus, the Spirit of God beareth witness unto my spirit[90] that such a one hath not the Spirit of Christ, and therefore is none of his[91]; for he is anathema[92] and no son of God, who is so ungrateful to the Crucified. Most lovable to me is he who spared not himself that he might gain me, nor can I find any way of repaying his most painful death other than by greatly loving him who first loved me so much as to lay down his life for me.[93] For whatever a man does in return for the death of Christ is inadequate from the point of view of sheer love.

(Ch. 8). Thou art the quail, who didst descend from on high into the Virgin's womb, that thou mightest fill us with flesh which could by no means harm us.[94] Thou art the hidden manna[95] of which we have received the measure of a gomor,[96] that is of perfection or consolation, because thou hast consoled thy people and wrought perfection for those who hope in thee in the sight of the sons of men.[97] Whoever has not tasted this manna has not yet experienced how sweet the Lord is. Thou art Samson, the strongest of men, who slew a thousand of his enemies with the jaw-bone of an ass[98]; in like manner didst thou lay low with the weapon of thy humanity him who has a thousand wiles for doing harm; just as when thou didst make a scourge of cords and therewith drive out of the temple the great crowd of people, buying and selling divers things.[99] Now Samson means 'strong sun',[100] which well applies to thee, since thou art the sun of justice which knows no setting, and thou art strong and mighty in battle as the Lord of hosts.[101] It was thou who didst shatter the brazen gates and bolts of iron,[102] and lift us out of the way of our sinfulness. What can it mean that Samson tied together the foxes' tails in order to burn the enemies' crops and vineyards, unless it be that thou didst likewise by means of the very snares and temptations of the demons destroy their own power? What follows confirms this interpretation. Thou art Samson, to whom it is said: 'Who is like unto thee amongst the strong ones, O Lord?'[103] And what are foxes' tails but the extremities of cunning animals, which well signify the wiles the demons employ against the Church of the elect, especially at the end of this life. To these the Bridegroom in the Canticle aptly refers when he makes the request: 'Catch us the little foxes which destroy the vineyards.'[104]

(Ch. 9).   Hence the Eternal spoke to the ancient one, God addressed the serpent, saying to the devil who appeared in that form, the enemy of the whole human race and head of all the reprobate: 'I will place enmities between thee and the seed of the woman. She shall crush thy head, and thou shalt lie in wait for her heel.'[105] What am I to understand by the seed of the woman, if not the sons of the Church, who are like olive saplings around the table of the Lord?[106] And what by the heel, if not the last days of the life of the elect, when, as has been said, the demons lie especially in wait for them, and would lead them astray,[107] were it not that God makes with temptation such issue[108] that they are able to resist, trampling upon the weapons of the most wicked one like ashes under the sole of the foot?[109] And thus may he who watched over their coming into the world, and saw to it that they should not remain without baptism, watch over their departure hence, and see to it that they be not seduced from the faith. What, moreover, am I to understand by the crops and vineyards of the Philistines, if not the power of the demons, who may well be called Philistines (that is 'falling when drunk'),[110] since of those demons who were intoxicated with conceit some fell from heaven into hell, and some into this misty atmosphere? But thou dost crush the power of these by means of their own schemes against the elect, for to them that love thee, who according to thy purpose are called to be saints,[111] all things work together for good; not only good works, but even sins. For example, one of the elect who is somewhat elated on account of an outstanding virtue is tempted by the devil to impurity and allowed to fall, so that the memory of so shameful a sin may for the future preserve him from pride, and give him rather, what is safer, a fellow-feeling for the lowly.

(Ch. 10).   Thou art the noble Jonathan, son of a great king, whose name means 'gift of the Lord',[112] for thou art the gift of God most high,[113] whose future coming Isaias foretold when he spoke these words of his own time: 'A child is born to us and a son is given to us.'[114] This, I repeat, is the best and perfect gift which came down to us from heaven from the Father of lights,[115] who so loved the world that he gave his only-begotten Son.[116] Thou, my Lord, art beauteous in form beyond the sons of men,[117] exceeding fair like Jonathan, and lovable above the love of women.[118] Thou hast made a covenant with the human race which no strife can ever break, for thy soul is knit with ours by thy love for man which exceeds that of a mother for her only son. Where have we proof of this? Verily, O Lord, thou who art so faithful to thy words that thou wilt not annul what comes forth from thy lips,[119] hast spoken by the prophet saying: 'Is it possible for a mother to forget her child so as not to have pity on the son of her womb? Even if she were to forget, yet will I not forget thee.'[120] As a sign of this indissoluble covenant thou didst put on the tunic of our humanity and clothe us with the garments of thy glory, as did Jonathan with David.[121]

Never dost thou fail, good Jesus, to take the greatest care of us, for whom thou didst prefer to die rather than permit us to remain in the power of the devil. The name of David is understood to mean 'strong of hand' or 'of attractive appearance'[122]: this double interpretation may not unfittingly be referred to the Church of the elect, since she is strong of hand and bears away the kingdom of God by violence; and she is of attractive appearance, so that the Lord desires her beauty, and her spouse speaks to her in the Canticle saying: 'Behold thou art beautiful, my love, behold thou art beautiful: thine eyes are as those of doves.'[123]

(Ch. 11). For when we provoked God the Father by our wicked deeds, when we corrupted our ways, and all man's thought was directed towards evil, so that there was none that did good, not even one[124]; when God repented that he had made man, and said that he would destroy him,[125] then thou, my Lord, thou didst stand forth in his presence to plead for reconciliation, lest we should altogether lose the land of our desires and be cast forth from before his face. Thus didst thou speak: 'Let thy wrath cease, O my Father, from thy people, that the thrones of those who have not stood in the truth may not remain unoccupied, and that thou mayest not destroy every living soul.[126] Let us by no means bring to naught in our city the likeness of those whom we have made to our own image and likeness,[127] but rather let thy wisdom prevail over the malice into which they have fallen through their proud self-love, desiring to become like gods, knowing good and evil.[128] Let it reach from thee, the end, for thou art both beginning and end, unto the end of all creation, that is to say man, who was created last of all, and let it dispose all things sweetly.[129] Since the devil has struck at the shield of knowledge, which is appropriated to me, this matter concerns me. Lo! here I am! send me.[130] I do not do this sadly, O Father, or under compulsion,[131] but rather I rejoice as a giant to run the way,[132] both because it is my delight to be with the sons of men,[133] and because I am stirred up to fight for man against the devil, who has persuaded the woman to covet knowledge. I will go then and capture him in his craftiness, and cleanse unto thee an acceptable people, pursuing good works,[134] that the whole world may know that there is no wisdom nor knowledge nor counsel against the Lord.'[135]

Thus, O my Lord, thou didst intercede with the Father for us, not with the sound of lips (for a spirit hath not flesh and bones[136]), but in the unspeakable way in which the Begotten Word holds intercourse with the Unbegotten Father; and thou didst reconcile us with our God and Father, when we were alienated from him,[137] not with words alone but with thine efficacious deeds. Not that entreaties such as these find any place within the Godhead, since all three Divine Persons have one will and are united in operation, therefore these things must be taken as said according to a human way of speaking.

(Ch. 12).

Thou art David who didst scatter with strong arm thy foes
and shatter death's barred gates to free thine own:

Thou didst slay the giant vaunting and the sons of Jacob
taunting; though thou hadst but sling and stone.

Thou like wood-worm undermining,[138] armed and battle not declining, victory didst nobly gain.

Philistinian ranks were saddened, Saul and his retainers gladdened by the trophies of the slain.

Warfare for us waging blithely, to the cross-top leaping lithely, hell's might thou didst overthrow.

Wondrous tones from thy harp ringing—thy wounds were its painful stringing—yield a tune man did not know.

Kindest Jesus then uphold us, when death's darkness doth enfold us, be our comfort and our stay.

That our ears anon may capture thy sweet strains in Heaven's rapture, make us now thy law obey.

Thou art Solomon supernal, who with crown and throne eternal reignest in thy majesty;

Lasting peace on us bestowing, thou art God the Son all-knowing, Second of the thrice-blest Three.

(Ch. 13). Thou art Christ, Son of the living God,[138a] who in obedience to the Father hast saved the world. Thou art a man of sorrows, not ignorant of our weakness; thou didst indeed take upon thyself our infirmities and bear our afflictions, when thou wast wounded for our sins and made sorrowful for our evil deeds: by thy bruises we have been healed.[139] Whosoever is on the Lord's side, let him join with me, that we may come to the visions of God.[140] I see thee, O good Jesus, nailed to the cross, crowned with thorns, given gall to drink, pierced with the lance, and for my sake dislocated in all thy limbs upon the gibbet of the cross. How greatly thou hast loved me, since whereas thou art thyself most good, for me thou hast desired to be reckoned among the wicked; being thyself most beautiful, for me thou hast desired to be accounted as a leper and the last of men; being thyself strong and powerful, for me thou didst allow thyself to be executed like a thief; being thyself wise, for me thou didst desire to be the butt of mocking words and gestures from those who stood around the cross, and so all that was within or without thee caused thee suffering for my sake. Alas! that head, an object of awe to angelic powers, is pierced with the sharpest thorns; the face upon which the angels desire to gaze[141] is spat upon by vile mouths; the hands which fashioned heaven and earth are pierced with sharp nails; the heart which knows all the secret things of God is laid bare when the side is opened; the belly from which flow living waters[141a] is contracted with hunger and pain; the back which supports heaven and earth is beaten and torn with stripes; the reins which extinguish all impurity are stripped and scourged; the legs which have wrought pleasure for men[142] are held fast by the point of the nails; the feet whose foot-stool is the universe are nailed to the cross; the soul, which from the first moment of its creation had full fruition of the Godhead, is sorrowful unto death.[143]

O soul, most blessed of all creatures, how happy was thy state, for no sooner thou didst exist than thou didst see God, being incorporated with the Godhead. Amongst all creatures thou dost hold the first place, since thou wast worthy to animate the King and Lord of heaven.[144] Henceforth I will call thee the seal of the likeness of God, full of all wisdom and comeliness. Do thou then, O Lady, who knoweth all things, persuade him, who can do all things, to have pity on thy handmaid, my soul.

(Ch. 14).   It is good, Lord Jesus, to recall yet further what was done to thee for our sake, to consider and behold thy reproach.[145] In thy head I perceive wondrous multiplicity of suffering, for in all thy five senses thou didst feel indescribable pain. Thou didst see thyself crucified and hanging between thieves, thy friends deserting thee, thine enemies gathering round, thy mother weeping, and the corpses of condemned criminals strewn round about; whatever met thy gaze was a source of pain and sorrow, of horror and dismay.

Thou didst hear threats, murmuring, sarcasm and taunts from the bystanders; threats, when they cried out: 'Away with him, away with him; crucify him'[146]; murmuring, when they said: 'He saved others, himself he cannot save',[146a] and some had said before that: 'He is good', while others said: 'No, he seduceth the multitude.'[147] Sarcasm, when the soldiers, bending their knees, greeted thee with: 'Hail, king of the Jews'[148]; for sarcasm is a covert sort of mockery, when one is ironically called something by the scoffer, other than what he believes to be true. They believed him indeed to be a criminal rather than the king of the Jews, and yet they spoke the truth although with false intent. Thou didst hear taunts, when they said: 'Vah! Thou who dost destroy the Temple and in three days rebuild it!'[149]

Thou didst taste bitterness, O Lord, when they gave thee gall for thy food, and in thy thirst gave thee vinegar to drink.[150] Thy nostrils, O Lord, breathed in the stench of the corrupting corpses of executed criminals lying round about. Thy sense of touch felt fierce pain in thy head, for the crown of thorns pierced it so grievously that thy blood flowed down in torrents through thy hair even to the ground. And so, good Lord, whatever thou didst look upon was terrible, whatever thou didst hear was horrible, whatever thou didst taste was bitter, whatever thou didst smell was putrid, and whatever thou didst touch was painful. From all this one can gather how much God should be loved by man, since he has deigned to suffer so much for him. In return for all this he asks nothing but that man should love him above all things.

(Ch. 15). One thing, O good Jesus, I would know of thee; namely what reward will be bestowed on thee for all that thou hast suffered for us, since we have nothing that we have not received from thee. All gold is but as a grain of sand in thy sight, and silver would be accounted mud in compensation for thy passion. What shall I render thee in return for all that thou hast rendered me? How shall I take the chalice of salvation, and in what way shall I call upon the name of the Lord,[151] since without thee I can do nothing, and no one can say 'Jesus is Lord' save by the Holy Spirit?[152] How, Lord Jesus, can that saying be true, that no evil goes unpunished nor any good unrewarded?[153] Where is the reward of God's Son, to whom we can give nothing, and from whom take nothing away, whose glory can neither be increased nor diminished? Tell me, I beseech thee, O Lord, what will be thy reward, since all that is is thine? Even if the Father has exalted thee and given thee a name which is above every name, that in the name of Jesus every knee should bow, of those who are in heaven, on earth and under the earth,[154] because thou wast made obedient to the Father even unto death, yet how does that affect us, or what great good has accrued to thee from it, since thy name was already holy and awe-inspiring,[155] so that every knee bent before it and all flesh confessed to it?[156] Perchance thou wilt answer: 'My hour is not yet come, nor is my reward in this world, but the hour cometh when I shall give sleep to my beloved ones, for whom I chose to suffer; I shall raise them up and incorporate them to myself in one body of which I am the head; and thus, when I shall have accomplished what I first purposed to do, this will be the reward which I wish to receive, the Son's inheritance, and the object of my desire.

(Ch. 16). 'There the love of the members for their head will be perfect and without measure, such as it cannot be here.[157] For there will be ineffable joy in the unspeakable delight of divine fruition, unsurpassable longing, unimaginable sweetness, all-embracing knowledge, power which can do all things, satiety which knows no distaste, security which has no fear. It is for these and other such like things that I suffered.'

What then, Lord, of the law, the prophets, the gospel, in all of which we are bidden to do so many and such great things in order to see thee? Answer me yet, I beg thee, Lord, this one question: what dost thou desire us to give thee in return for the sufferings thou hast endured for us? Speak, Lord, for thy servants listen, ready to receive the engrafted word which is able to save their souls.[158] 'If thou desirest to know this plainly, call thy husband, that thou mayest understand aright.[159] Let him who hath ears to hear, hear what Christ saith now to the churches.[160]

(Ch. 17). 'Behold the inheritance of the Lord and reward of the son is the fruit of the womb.[161] It is this that I desire above all things, nor is there anything amongst men which I so long for.' Good Jesus, what is this that thou desirest so ardently and claimest as thy special reward? Does not every man, every womb, every fruit belong to thee, and in fine are not all things thine both visible and invisible? What is this fruit of the womb that thou dost so eagerly demand? Something desirable and inestimably precious is here implied, which, because we are as yet without understanding, is hidden from our eyes,[162] until the declaration of thy words give understanding to little ones. O kind and lovable Lord Jesus, tell us plainly what thou meanest by the fruit of the womb.

Thou answerest: 'In all thy house is naught that I so covet as thy heart; not that fleshly object but its love. This is the fruit that I desire, which is more precious to me than all riches, and naught that is desirable can be compared with it. There is nothing more precious within thee, and therefore it may with reason be called the fruit of the womb. It is for this that I ask, it is this that I prize beyond all other offerings; to dwell within it is my delight, and I suffered for thee solely that thou mightest give it to me.'

Good Jesus, I grant what thou askest, and wish to give thee what thou desirest; but thou wilt never have my heart, unless thou first give me thyself, partly because I will not hand over my treasure except in exchange for something better, and partly because without thee I can do nothing.

(Ch. 18).   I know well, O Lord, that thou desirest my whole self when thou askest for my heart, and I seek thy whole self when I beg for thee. I know too, O Lord, that thou wishest to possess me entirely, in order that thou mayest be entirely possessed thyself, and this thou dost for my sake, not for thine own. For thou who hast all things, hast no need of my goods.[163] I believe that thou requirest this thing from me as a gift, because thou knowest that it is at the disposal of my free-will, for no one loveth against his will. It is as if thou didst say: 'Give me what I have given thee.'

'If I have not this, I am not Lord of all. The angels love me, and the evil spirits are subject to me; I wish to be loved by man, and so to rejoice in universal dominion. I am most covetous and exceeding jealous, because I wish to have all and to be loved above all, and if any one turn away his heart from me, I will harden him, and his love shall be changed into avarice; I will bring a horrible death upon him, and plunge him into Hell, so that he who once refused to love me will anon begin to blaspheme with the evil spirits. But on the other hand, if any

one love me, he shall be loved by the Father, and I will love
him and manifest myself to him,[164] for by his own love he
purchases to himself the fruits of my passion.'

(Ch. 19).   Why is it, Lord, that thou hatest those who are
covetous, when thou thyself art most covetous, unless it be
that as long as they are merely covetous, they are not most
covetous? For were they so they would aspire to the supreme
good, than which nothing greater nor better can be desired,
since it is all in all. I do wish to give what thou desirest, O
Lord, if I can have what I desire. I fully grant, O Jesus, what
thou askest, and long to give thee what thou wouldst have. Do
thou therefore, who hast first enabled me to will this, so further
it by thy assistance that I may accomplish it. To will is present
with me, and that through thy gift, but to accomplish I find
not,[165] unless thou reach out to me the hand of thy mercy, so
that by my act of will and thy assistance, when thou hast taken
what is thine, I may love thee above all things, O Lord.

Enkindle, I beseech thee, O Lord, the light of our understanding, and pour forth love into our hearts,[166] that I may be
able to love thee perfectly and praise thee worthily.[167] Create
a clean heart within me, O God,[168] so that it may become thine
abode and the resting-place of the Holy Spirit. I know, O Lord,
I know indeed that thou art beautiful and so it is presumptuous
of me to invite majesty so great into the dwelling of so defiled
a heart; but I invite thee in order that thou mayest cleanse it,
and afterwards, I beg thee if it please thee, depart not from me,
and even unto old age and grey hairs leave me not.[169]

(Ch. 20).   Thy coming, O good Jesus, is exceeding sweet
and thine embraces greatly to be desired; thy kisses are as
honey and thy presence so desirable that, if thou wert to remain, this earth would become heaven, and a heart of flesh the
bridal-chamber of the only-begotten Son of God. But alas!
How true are the words: 'My spirit shall not remain long in
man, seeing that he is but flesh'!'[170] Nor were it any wonder if
he, in whose eyes the heavens themselves are not pure,[171]
should refuse to dwell in our houses of clay. Much less are we

worthy, who, defiled with the filth of our sins, embrace the dung[172]; even if he do at times out of his goodness enter under our roof[173] to abide with us. This he does especially according to that operation whereby he enables us to tafte the firft-fruits of the Spirit, by breaking for us a little of the bread which is himself, and saying: 'Tafte and see that the Lord is sweet.'[174]

Thou canft, O good Jesus, moft clearly be recognized in the breaking of this bread,[175] which no one else breaks as thou doft. For thou doft visit the soul with such joy, and fill it with such ineffable delight and indescribable love, that for one who loves such favours the enjoyment of so gracious a visit from such a gueft, were it only for the space of a day, would surpass in delight all the love of women and a whole world full of riches. This is not surprising, since it is a sort of beginning of eternal joys, a sign of divine predeftination and pledge of eternal salvation; it is a grace rendering us pleasing to God, and beftows on us a new name, which no one knows save he who receives it,[176] and apart from the sons and daughters of God none can have a share in it.

(Ch. 21). This it was which made the martyrs triumph over tyrants, fearing neither fire, beafts, nor the sword; this too made the confessors overcome the devil, and won the victory of martyrdom for the frail sex.[177] Therefore, good Lord, since union with thee is evidently so desirable for the soul that wishes to love God above all things, do thou pour forth into our hearts the warmth of thy love, so that loving thee in all and above all, we may deserve to experience within us those visits of thine, which surpass all worldly delights.[178]

Moreover I entreat thee, good Jesus, by the omnipotent might of the undivided Trinity, by the flesh which thou didft assume from the inviolate Virgin, by thy precious blood which was shed for many unto the remission of sins,[179] by the merits and prayers of the moft blessed Virgin Mary and of all the saints, and by all that can moft effectively persuade thee to grant the prayers of thy suppliants, or will persuade thee in the future; as well as by all that thou knoweft can moft powerfully influence thee to accede to the petitions of those that entreat thee (if ever it should please thee to reveal such a thing to any living person); vouchsafe, O Lord, that whosoever shall devoutly and carefully complete this meditation for love of thy name and in memory of thy bitter passion, may be made a partaker of that blood, and may become one of those for whom it has been shed unto the remission of sins. I beg thee also to bestow such grace on this composition, that as often as the whole or half of it, (namely from the sentence: 'Thou art Christ, Son of the living God')[180] be read in the heart or meditated upon (for meditation even without labial utterance is in reality speech of the heart), it may more and more enable the reader to understand about thy passion, so that he may reach the love of God; I mean that love with which a man loves God, not that whereby he is loved by God.

(Ch. 22). For God hateth none of those things which he has made,[181] although he may be said to hate many, as for instance Esau. The reason why God is said to hate such men is that he foresees, or knows beforehand, that they will do such things as to merit divine hatred; it is not that God, who is immutable, is really subject to such passions, for he is ever the same, and with him there is no change,[182] but God's hatred, strictly speaking, means that grace is either withdrawn or not imparted. He has mercy and bestows it on whom he will, and on whom he will not he bestows it not, but hardens him, or rather permits him to be hardened; in exalting the one he is lovable, in humbling the other he is terrible; but in neither case is he culpable, for it is lawful for him to do whatsoever he pleases, and he enjoys no less liberty than the potter, who out of the same lump fashions one vessel unto honour and another unto dishonour.[183] If one should seek a reason for the latter, it is said that the craftsman wishes it so, and if one asks why God gives to one what he does not give to another, the answer is: 'because he wills it'. The Will of God is independent of any cause, since it is itself the first cause of all things, visible and invisible, which the Creator has made. These things are indeed so, and yet, thanks to the wonderful workings of divine providence, God neither condemns anyone unjustly nor saves anyone except by his grace; nor does he act less well when he punishes the one than when he bestows the kingdom upon the other. However, I never did think I should find means of understanding these things, nor shall I ever expect to, until I enter into the holy place of God, and understand from their final fate[184] what has been revealed to me in this word; this alone I understand now, that it is reasonable for God to do with his creature whatsoever he pleases.

(Ch. 23). I am therefore compelled to exclaim with the apostle: 'O the depths of the riches of the wisdom and knowledge of God; how incomprehensible are his judgements and unsearchable his ways!'[185] How terrible, I would add, is he in his counsels over the sons of men,[186] who prefer vanity to God, as they seek after falsehood; whose mouth has spoken vanity and whose right hand is the right hand of iniquity.[187]

Yet how benignant and kind is he to those who are upright of heart, who have not forsaken the spring of living water,[188] nor departed from God, their Saviour[189]; but rather are numbered amongst that people whose God is the Lord. These know by experience that jubilation,[190] of which I have spoken above, which can arise from no other source than an understanding of the works of Christ, whence David says: 'I will exult in the works of thy hands.'[191] This exultation springs from loving confidence, for a mind free from anxiety is like a perpetual feast,[192] and fear does not abide in the charity[193] which grows out of frequent meditation on our Lord's passion.

There is in truth no other reason why God is not loved by man, save that man does not know or take to heart what God has done for him. It is because of this that we specially beseech God in these words of the litany: 'From blindness of heart, O Lord deliver us.' Blindness of this kind will lead one who suffers from it now into exterior darkness in the future, and if anyone fails to guard himself against it carefully, it is to be feared that he will perish for ever. The opposite of this blindness or ignorance is that knowledge by which the faithful know Jesus Christ, and him crucified.[194] Give me, good Lord, this knowledge, for its light cannot be put out,[195] and will not suffer the soul to walk in darkness. It is an infinite treasure to men, and those who have made use of it have become sharers in the friendship of God, for knowledge of him is inseparably linked with love of him, whom no one has ever known without loving.

(Ch. 24). Consider then, O man, what God has done for you, and be not ungrateful to your Saviour, who, although he is sweet in all things, and his mercies are upon all his works,[196] will yet be manifested to you as incomparably sweeter because, when you were nothing, he created you out of nothing, a noble creature, to his own image[197]; after that he appointed angels to keep you; that is, a good angel to guard you, and an evil spirit to try you. Think not that he will make little account of that which he has entrusted to an angel to guard.

Moreover he created all other beings to serve you, desiring that nothing should be superior to you save himself alone, and in order to show you still further the exceeding greatness of his kindness and condescension, he emptied himself, taking the form of a servant, and was found in appearance just like other men.[198] He who in the beginning created heaven and earth,[199] was afterwards seen upon the earth, and conversed with men[200] for thirty-two years and three months. Even this would not satisfy him, but he must needs be put to death in the cruellest and most shameful way for the salvation of your soul.

O man, ungrateful towards your Saviour, whosoever you are, who, forgetting your Lord and Maker,[201] prefer the creature to the Creator; I shall set upon you with words: let me contend with you. If there is nothing in human dealings more detestable than ingratitude, so that one man is manifestly ungrateful to another if he forgets a benefit received, or ill requites his benefactor, what shall I say of him who is ungrateful towards Christ?

(Ch. 25). 'To begin my contention with the words of the master: "Whosoever loves not the Lord Jesus, let him be anathema." '[202] Take Bernard's word for it, not mine, you who are such that, did not God in his mercy and kindness always chastize the sinner less than he deserves, there would be no torment in hell adequate to punish your sin of ingratitude. For this is an evil, admittedly worse than any other, and if it abides with a man until death, and he remains unrepentant in spite of all, it is worse than the malice of the devil, for God never assumed the latter's nature in personal union, nor was he, neither will he ever be, crucified for him.

What do you say, ungrateful man? Why love gold more than God, silver more than Chrift, vanity more than the Trinity, the creature more than the Creator? Do you think that he who formed the ear does not hear, or that he who fashioned the eye is not watching what you do?[203] Do you suppose that, although he is silent now and holds his peace, he will not speak out like one in labour?[204] Do you imagine that God is a liar, that he is asleep or in an inn,[205] that you defy him in this ftiff-necked fashion? You muft surely say in your heart: 'there is no God',[206] since you aft thus, 'and there is no one who will require these things at my hands'.[206a] Or, if you do believe that there is a God who searches out such things and judges them,[207] where will you hide from the face of his anger in the day of the wrath of the Lord?[208] Is there anyone to proteft you in hell until his wrath has passed;[209] or have you made a compaft with hell, so that you can dwell with devouring fire and its flame hurt you not; with everlasting burning,[210] and the smell of fire not be in you? Why is your malice not enough for you? Can you not die alone in sin without wearying the whole Trinity? You compel the Father to invent a new torment for you in hell, you provoke the Son to come to judgement to be avenged of you, and, to the beft of your ability, you quench the Holy Spirit, for ingratitude is a sin which, according to Bernard, quenches the source of piety.[211]

What will you say, ungrateful man, on the day of judgement, when the Lord will visit upon you all your iniquity? What will you do, son of eternal death, prepared for burning and fuel of fire,[212] to escape his hands, when there is none that can snatch or be snatched out of his hand?[213] If you ascend into heaven, there you will find him whom you flee; if you descend into hell, he is there; if you take wings in the morning and dwell in the uttermoft parts of the sea, even thence will his hand retrieve you and his right hand faften upon you,[214] and he will drag you before the judge, that you may underftand that there is no place where God is not. Flight then is impossible. What of appearing before the judge? Verily it will be unbearable, both for terror and for shame, for none can endure his wrath, and it will be less shameful to be called by him a devil than an ungrateful Christian.

On the other hand, if I be found pleasing to the Saviour on that day, I would not change my nature with any in the order of the Seraphim, even though I be called the least in the kingdom of heaven, for once there I shall be blessed, and it will be well with me in accordance with my rank and merits. But when I fix my inward gaze upon the circle of the divine life, and behold my own nature so united to God in personal union, that a man should think it not robbery to be equal with God,[215] whose good pleasure it is to dwell in him bodily according to the whole fullness of the Godhead[216]; when I see flesh and blood sitting upon the throne of the Trinity, how greatly do you think shall I then rejoice with him in his glory and exult in God my Jesus![217] For whatever I see bestowed upon him there, I shall regard as done to me; although he is God, whose nature I do not share, yet he is also man with a nature like unto mine. Which of the angels would dare to say to him: 'Thou art my brother as well as my God'? Not one of them. It is enough for them to adore the man Christ, their Lord and ours.

(Ch. 26). Cursed indeed is he who does not trust in this man nor establish him as his arm,[218] through whom we have confidence and access to the Father.[219] Whosoever he is, he will undoubtedly have to bear judgement, and that from no other judge than him towards whom he has shown ingratitude, for he has been appointed by God judge of the living and the dead.[220] Perchance someone will ask me in what this ingratitude consists which is so terrible that it surpasses in enormity the very malice of the devil. My answer is: suppose one were to partake of the Sacraments of the Church, taste the sweetness of the grace of the Holy Spirit, and afterwards turn back by loving the creature more than the Creator, or, what is worse, forget God altogether and foolishly say in one's heart: 'There is no God',[221] or even be inflamed with fires of envy against the grace by which one was reconciled. Augustine indeed tells us that this is the sin against the Holy Ghost, concerning which John says in his epistle: 'I say not that anyone should pray.'[222]

St Paul in the epiſtle to the Hebrews declares that it is impossible for a man of that kind to be renewed unto repentance: 'For it is impossible for those who have once been illuminated, have even taſted the heavenly gift, become partakers of the Holy Ghoſt, and moreover have taſted the good word and the virtues of the world to come and are fallen, to be renewed again unto penance.'[223]

Added to which, the misery of the sin is manifeſtly so great that it cannot be hidden even from men, for it follows necessarily that one who is not in God's grace is not considered pleasing by men either. For such a one can be speedily recognized by his fruits, which are disputes, rivalries, angry outburſts, quarrels, disagreements, self-conceit, loathing for hearing or speaking about God, dislike of being contradiɛted, which is the hall-mark of pride, readiness to give away nothing or very little for the love of God,—and even that grudgingly, of necessity, and in such a way as to provoke the poor,—greed for money and miserliness.[224] These are all marks by which to recognize the man who loves what is transitory more than God.

(Ch. 27). I believe, however, that nothing is so displeasing to God as not to love him. To give away one's possessions or to undergo even martyrdom itself is of no avail without love of God, to which we are obliged by the firſt commandment of the decalogue. Whence blessed Gregory says: 'If you omit what is of obligation, whatever you offer will be unacceptable to God.'[225] For he who believes not in God is displeasing to him, he who hopes not in God is ſtill more displeasing, but he who does not love God is moſt displeasing of all.

Do not then, O man, love anything or any things or all things together more than God, or as much as God, but love him above all; love not yourself, nor your neighbour, nor the world, nor the angels, nor the saints, nor the Virgin Mary herself, not Peter, nor Paul as you love Jesus Chriſt; for Peter was not crucified for you, neither did you receive baptism in the name of Paul.[226] If anyone should say to you: 'I belong to Peter, to whom do you?', answer: 'To Chriſt: they are the miniſters of Chriſt, and so am I, I know no God but Jesus.'[227] For whoever loves this or that holy man or woman more than the Lord Jesus is deceived by the appearance of holiness, and falls into the abyss of idolatry, because he sets up as a god for himself whatever he loves most. He alone deserves to be loved by us above all things, who alone deigned to suffer for our salvation.

(Ch. 28).   'But', you will object, 'the Church sings of God's Mother:

> Of thy Son, in degradation
> Dying under condemnation,
> Love bade thee for our salvation
> Suffer with the paschal Lamb.'[228]

My answer is, that since the Church sings this (although I do not know how authoritative the composer is), I would like to add a gloss, or assign a different meaning to the words from that which they superficially imply; so that the sense would be: 'love of thy Son, in degradation dying for our salvation under condemnation, bade thee suffer the sword of sorrow with the paschal Lamb'. Or alternatively: 'for the sake of thy salvation, love of thy Son bade thee suffer, having compassion with him on the cross', and because thy salvation is our salvation, since through thee we merited to receive the author of life,[229] not without reason is it stated immediately after the words 'for our salvation' that thou didst suffer. Or else, because a sword of sorrow pierced thy soul[230] through thy compassion for him who suffered for our salvation, and so, in a certain indirect way, thou didst suffer for our salvation. It was to restore this salvation that thy Son desired to die both for thy salvation and ours, and his passion gave thee cause for sorrow.

No one else's passion was of avail to himself for salvation, until that Lamb was sacrificed who took away the sins of the world; far less was it of avail to others, for all were sinners and had need of Christ's passion,[231] nor was there any man or woman who could say: 'I am so free from stain of sin that I have no need of Christ's passion.'

Therefore do not by your love make for yourself a god of anything save him alone who loved us so greatly when we did not as yet exist. I do not forbid the love of saints, but I do desire that right order should be kept in loving them.

(Ch. 29). Since for Christ's sake I have disputed at length with the ungrateful man, the duty of kindness now demands that I should soothe him with the consolation of the scriptures, lest he fall into despair, and should expound to him the very same writings with which I terrified him; and also, if I can, I mean to show him how to flee the wrath of the judge who is to come.

To begin, however, with the words of the doctors Augustine and Gregory: 'No one is more sick than he who knows not that he is sick', as Augustine says,[232] and according to Gregory: 'the physician who has not endured sickness along with the sick man, knows not how to restore him to health'.[233] So I am going to tell you that I myself am ungrateful to God, and have long been so, for I do not keep his commandments, nor did I keep them formerly as I should have done, but often followed my inclinations with regard to the desires of the flesh, and turned aside from the unchangeable good to what was changeable. Alas! how often did not the serpent deceive me, and concupiscence corrupt my heart,[234] which from the time of my youth proved to be a vessel full of all vileness and sin, for I loved the creature more than the Creator, to my own great detriment. But now I blush before thee, O Lord, and am covered with confusion,[235] because I have so long been ungrateful to thee, turning my back upon thine embraces, biting when thou wouldst have kissed me, fleeing when thou didst pursue me, and repaying thy benefits with evil.

(Ch. 30). See, brother, what a beam I left lodged in my own eye, when I hastened to remove the splinter from my brother's eye.[236] And though I have done all these things, yet I shall not despair of God's mercy[237] as long as I breathe in the Spirit of the Lord and the breath of the Almighty does not depart from me. So do not you despair either, for behold now is the acceptable time, now is the day of salvation, that, giving offence to no man,[238] a man may confess his sins and receive penance for their remission. For to despair of God's mercy would indeed be a sin against the Holy Ghost and unforgivable blasphemy.

There is no sin, nor any number of sins, for which a man cannot obtain forgiveness, if he truly repents in this life and confesses his wickedness.

As for that sin of which we are speaking, namely the sin against the Holy Ghost, which the Truth says shall be forgiven neither here nor hereafter, I would say that Christ declares that it is not forgiven here, not because it cannot be forgiven here, if anyone repents of it before death and begs pardon; but it is said not to be forgiven here, because seldom or never is forgiveness for it sought; in the same way men are wont to say: 'he did not get it because he did not ask for it'. The very fact that a man despairs means that he is hardened against seeking forgiveness, for no one, unless he is a fool or jesting, seeks that which he despairs of being able to obtain. Anyone who begs forgiveness does not despair of the possibility of its being granted to him. And on the other hand if anyone does not beg forgiveness it is because he does despair.

(Ch. 31).   There are, moreover, two other reasons why men who fall into despair are often prevented from seeking forgiveness; namely because that sin assails them especially at the end of life, when the short span left allows no time for repentance, and because the pains of death are so acute that they prevent them from thinking of such a thing. Hence John in his epistle calls it by another name, the 'sin unto death'[239] because, as I said before, it molests a man when at the point of bodily death, which is the first death, and also leads him on, unrepentant, to eternal death, which is the second death following on this life. So the Apostle says: 'Let no one pray' concerning it, for there is no redemption in Hell,[240] and we should not pray for the damned; for this reason Augustine declares: 'If I knew my father to be in Hell, I would not pray for him any more than for the devil.'[241]

And now, as for what the Apostle says in Hebrews: 'It is impossible for those who have once, etc. . . . to be renewed again unto penance', my answer is: according to the gloss, to be renewed means to be baptized, for just as Christ died once on account of our sins, so we have been baptized once in his death, and just as it is impossible for him that is immortal to die, so it is impossible for us to be baptized again unto penance or in place of penance, even though we have fallen back again into sins, similar to those which we committed before baptism, unless we wish to 'crucify Christ again and make a mockery of the Son of God', to use the words in which the selfsame Apostle writes of these things.[242]

(Ch. 32). Hence the sacrament of penance has been instituted in the Church for the sake of those who fall again, and, because it does not confer a character, it can be repeated, except in the case of solemn penance: but this opinion I leave to those who dispute about it.[243] On the other hand, we confess but one baptism for the remission of sins, which does confer a character, and cannot be repeated.

The interpretation of the word 'renewed' rests upon the authority of the Apostle writing to Titus; this being what he had in mind when he said: 'The kindness and humaneness of God our Saviour has appeared to us; not for any works of justice we have done, but according to his mercy he has saved us by the cleansing of regeneration',[244] to which he immediately adds 'of renewal', for the sake of those who, having fallen after baptism, did not believe that it was possible to be restored to salvation save by baptism. Let this suffice for understanding the texts. It now remains to be seen how to escape the wrath of the Lamb,[245] who will show us which road to take, and whither to flee.

(Ch. 33). The Lord's forerunner puts the first question to those approaching him, when he says: 'Generation of vipers, who will show you to flee from the wrath to come?'[246] The royal prophet replies in the psalm, addressing Christ: 'Thou hast given a signal to them that fear thee, that they may flee from before the bow, that thy beloved may be delivered.'[247] We know then that it was he who gave the sign who showed the way. What way will he point out to us? Assuredly none other than himself, since he says: 'I am the way; by me if any man enter in he shall be saved.'[248] What is our goal? Whither

are we to flee? Without doubt to him who says: 'Come to me
all ye who labour and are heavily burdened.'[249] What a marvel-
lous decree, to flee from someone through himself and to himself! The reason for this is that it is impossible to flee from an
angry God save to a conciliated God,[250] for by the very fact
that you fly to him you reconcile him with yourself. In this way,
and in this way alone, can you prevail over sovereign goodness,
by committing yourself wholly to his will. For great-hearted
lords are wont to forgive everything when their offenders
present themselves before them of their own accord, giving
their lords full liberty to deal with them as they will.

(Ch. 34).   Two things deter men from approaching kings—
low condition and a sense of shame; but the prophet excludes
both in the words: 'Come ye to him and be ennobled, and your
faces shall not be confounded.'[251] Nothing is truer than that as
we approach God we are ennobled (just as the lepers were
cleansed as they went to show themselves to the priests),[252] and
our faces will not be confounded, because there is no confusion
to them that trust in thee, O Lord.[253] We must, however, note
carefully what sort of people the prophet is addressing when he
declares that the Lord has given a signal 'that they should flee
from before the bow'.[254] Obviously he is speaking to God-
fearing men, not to those who are proud, envious, ill-tempered
or slothful; not to adulterers, but to those 'who fear thee'.
Many men do indeed fear hell, the loss of temporal goods and
suchlike, and yet do not turn away from sin. But such men,
since they do not fear God, receive no sign 'to flee from before
the bow'. Only upon those who fear thee, O Lord, will the
sun of justice arise; only for them is there safety in thy wings,
so that they may be hidden beneath their shadow until iniquity
pass away.[255]

Thou hast given a signal. What signal? To be sure, that they
may flee from before the bow, that thy beloved may be delivered. What bow is this but that which the Lord has long
drawn, preparing therein deadly shafts, from the days of Noe,
when the flood came and destroyed every living soul from the
face of the earth, except the eight and the creatures that were
with them in the ark.[256] After that he drew his bow through

wars and uprisings, plagues and famine, earthquakes and human slaughter, until the time appointed by the Father, when God sent his Son,[257] who did not keep secret from us the signs which will precede the appearance of his bow, but said: 'There shall be signs in the sun and moon and stars, and on earth distress of nations because of the confusion of the sound of the sea and waves' and so forth.[258]

(Ch. 35). But he has shown us by many other signs in the law and the prophets, in the Gospel and by what we daily behold with our own eyes, that there is no long interval between his drawing his bow and releasing the string. O how bitter will be the releasing of his shaft, since the drawing of his bow is known to be so harsh! Truly from the way in which he draws it we can learn that when he lets his shaft fly, neither man nor devil, heaven, earth nor sea will be able to stand its violence when it strikes. I will fly then from before the bow, whose signs, thanks to the Lord's instructions, we have now recognized.

There is one thing, however, which still perplexes me: seeing that these signs are announced to the wicked as well as to the good, to the reprobate as well as to the elect, and are read out in church, what is that signal, clearly unique and singular, which is spoken of as being specially given to those that fear God, that his beloved may be delivered? And, since his beloved alone are to be delivered, why is the signal given to those that fear God?

Can it be that a signal to fly is necessary for those who fear, whereas knowledge of God itself implies deliverance for those who love him? Or is it that the beloved and those who fear God are actually one and the same, for blessed are all they who fear God, and their fear, being filial, is not cast out by perfect love, but has power to remain forever?[259] Since, however, fear means one thing and love another, it was fitting that one who shared the divine secrets should say that warning to fly is given to those who fear God, and that he should announce their deliverance to the beloved.

(Ch. 36). Thou hast given a signal—what signal? Why not more than one? Can that one alone be enough for those who fear thee, that they may fly from before the bow? Yes certainly, not only from before the bow, but also in the meantime it will avail to save us from all tribulation and distress, and from every diabolical temptation. O wonderful sign, stirring men up to the love of God, which the Lord raised up amidst the nations, gathering together the dispersed of Israel![260] O sign of especial love and surpassing sweetness, full of all the fidelity of love, which many see and few understand! All day long it is manifest in church, and yet few are stirred up by it to love. Why so? Because the fact is that he who is of God understands the sign of God; therefore they do not understand, because they are not of God;[261] but rather from among those of whom it is said that 'seeing they may not see, and hearing may not understand'.[262] O saving signal, cleansing the wound and restoring health! What a singular sign, I say, unique and without its like; nothing resembling it can be found by land or sea. What a sign, I repeat, what a precious and wonderful sign, divine and triumphant! By means of it the devil was overcome and the world delivered from his tyranny. Thou hast, then, given a signal. What is a signal?

(Ch. 37).   A signal is an intimation or an indication to do something. For if anyone makes you a sign, he indicates to you silently what he has done, or what he wants you to do. I beseech thee, Lord, teach me this sign! For I have learnt many signs from monks, by means of which when for silence' sake they do not speak they signify to one another with their fingers what they want or what they themselves have done; but all those together do not amount to thy signal, for I have learnt them all in vain if I should happen to be ignorant of this one. I beseech thee, O Lord, show me what this sign is, and hide not this word from thy servant.

I do not believe, O Lord, that because of my insistence in entreating thee for this sign I shall be like those to whom thou didst say: 'This perverse generation seeketh a sign.'[263] Nay rather! I think it will be pleasing in thine eyes, if for my own instruction I ask thee to reveal to me what thou meanest by this sign, since I do not know what thou wishest to convey by it. Should I, however, have the intention of hiding from my brethren what thou speakest in my ear, then indeed let this sign be far from my understanding!

What am I to say? Shall I keep silence or speak? Hold my peace or give utterance? For what thou showest me is exceedingly profound, and being defiled I dare not speak of such matters. Speak thou then for me, O Lord, this time, and let there be a good word in thy mouth, which may bring grace to those that hear it. Truly I would not restrain my lips, were they not defiled from yesterday and the day before,[264] so that they are not worthy to expound so great a mystery.

(Ch. 38). Would that my longing might imprint its own characters on the hearts of them that hear, just as the hand that writes presents them to the eyes of readers; but this belongs to the Trinity alone, the husbandman; for neither is he anything who plants, nor he who waters, but God who gives the increase.[265] Since however this exceeds the angelic nature, it exceeds our human weakness too, and belongs to absolutely no one but the divine husbandman, the Trinity; I reproach myself for having spoken foolishly, and am not worthy to be heard for my folly.[266] It is enough for me that I have this task to perform; may the Lord open the ear of whomsoever he please, and the Spirit breathe where he will.[267] The tongue of the teacher labours in vain, if the Spirit is not within to teach; his instruction knows no delay and no effort,[268] nor does a slow-witted mind obstruct it.

'Thou hast given', I repeat, 'a sign to them that fear thee, that they may flee from before the bow.' Why does it say: 'Thou hast given', since that sign had not yet been given when David prophesied, for Christ had not yet appeared in the flesh; unless it be that, while they are prophesying, the prophets, who foresee what is to come, have their sight united to that of God, in whose eyes even future events have already taken place? Or did he foretell these things in the past tense in order to indicate thereby that it is just as impossible for a prophet's words not to be fulfilled as it would be for something that has happened not to have happened? Thus David is wont to employ the past tense, in for instance: 'they gave me gall for my food'[269] and other similar passages which, as no one doubts, were spoken of Christ.

I beseech thee now, O Lord, tell us what this signal is that thou haſt given to them that fear thee, that thy beloved may be delivered. I shall speak in thy name, Lord, leſt my own authority should seem worthless; I should rightly be held in contempt if I announced this as coming from myself and not from thee. To the beſt of my belief thou answereſt that the sign which I have sought is this:

(Ch. 39). 'All day long I ſtretch out my hands on the cross towards thee, O man, to embrace thee, I bow down my head to kiss thee when I have embraced thee, I open my side to draw thee into my heart after this kiss, that we may be two in one flesh.[270] There can be safety for thee nowhere else but in me, when the day of wrath and judgement comes. See, I have shown thee the sign thou didſt beg; know then how much I love, and fly quickly to me.'

What love and goodness, what generous fidelity! O treasure of riches and refuge of delight! O haven of salvation and shield of protection! What shall I say, what words can I utter? Who ever heard the like?[271] Who would not marvel at such graciousness? Who would not be amazed at such condescension in majeſty so great? Lo, he offers us embraces and kisses who by a mere word created the universe.[272]

(Ch. 40). Even so is it with mothers who love their little children tenderly; if these happen to be at a diſtance from them, and want to run to them quickly, they are wont to ſtretch out their arms and bend down their heads. Then the little ones, taught in a natural way by this geſture, run and throw themselves into their mothers' arms, and the latter beſtow trinkets on them, or, if they are not yet weaned, give them the breaſt.

Chriſt our Lord does the same with us. He ſtretches out his hands to embrace us, bows down his head to kiss us, and opens his side to give us suck; and though it is blood which he offers us to suck, we believe that it is health-giving and sweeter than honey and the honey-comb.[273] Do not wean me, good Jesus, from the breaſts of thy consolation[274] as long as I live in this world, for all who suffer this abide in death, as thou thyself didst testify in the gospel saying: 'Unless you eat the flesh of the Son of man and drink his blood, you shall not have life in you.'[275]

Perhaps someone will say to me: 'I do not agree that this is the explanation of the sign; for he would not have stretched out his arms if he had not been fixed to the cross with nails, he would not have bowed down his head but for the fact that his soul left his body, and his side would not have been opened had it not been pierced by the lance.'

(Ch. 41). My answer is this: Man liveth not by bread alone but by every word which proceedeth from the mouth of God.[275a] His words are spirit and life,[276] profoundly hidden and fraught with manifold mysteries, so that if a whole world of men should choose to apply themselves to discussing them exhaustively they could never succeed in doing so, for like the loaves with which our Lord fed five thousand men, there would still remain subject matter for those men who first wished to study them zealously, and, should new commentators appear, enough to fill more than ten baskets with books.

How then can the work of our salvation which our Lord has wrought and revealed to us be so straitened as to be mastered by one mind alone, since the voice of deeds is no less eloquent than that of words? God forbid!

Who would ever assert that the hands of the Almighty could be fixed to the cross in such a way that he remained thus hanging simply by reason of the nails, as though he died against his will? This is not true, for he was offered up because he so willed.[277] Or what prater dare likewise say that the hands of God could be so transfixed by the nails that he would be unable to bend his arms—he who has done all things whatsoever and whensoever he pleased?[278] Or who would declare that when the soul departed the head which was venerated by the angelic powers must of necessity sink down, as though God who upholds all things and is upheld by none were not present with it?

All such ideas are frivolous, and ill become any Christian. On the contrary, the truth is that he did all these things for the sake of mankind, and wished to hang thus in order to show

forth a sign to those who feared him. Nevertheless if we understand the sign in a material way, we shall be far from following
the course of discretion; for we read that Judas betrayed our
Lord with a kiss,[279] and elsewhere that Jesus embraced a
child.[280]

(Ch. 42). Since, however, he who revealed these things to
us is in heaven, whither no one can ascend bodily to embrace
or kiss him or do any such thing, nor will he descend thence
until he comes in judgement, it remains for us to seek another
interpretation of this sign, for fear we too might gain no profit
from it.

Allegorically, then, I might take Christ's outstretched arms
and hands to stand for the law and the prophets, and justifiably
so, for the law of Moses was written by the hand of God, and
Scripture tells us that the holy hand of the Lord was upon the
prophets.[281] We can see how he stretched out his hand to the
latter, as though giving them a hint, when at various times and
in divers ways God, speaking of old to the fathers through
the prophets in an obscure and enigmatical way,[282] suggested
to them what they ought to do rather than telling them plainly,
for the letter killeth, and the law brought no one to perfection,
until he who had first given the law came to give a blessing.[283]

But since neither the law nor prophecy were given in vain,
it was through them that God drew to his own embrace the
Jewish people and also all the gentiles who desired to be cir-
cumsized, that is to say the peculiar people whose God he
especially declared himself to be, saying: 'I am the God of
Abraham, the God of Isaac and the God of Jacob.'[284] David
pays splendid tribute to them in the psalm when he breaks out
with the words: 'Famed in Judea is God, in Israel great is his
name.'[285] God, then, bent down his head and bestowed a kiss
upon us, when he bowed the heavens and came down,[286]
assuming human nature in a personal union.

(Ch. 43). I beg you, reader, to heed carefully what I am
about to say, that you may know the ineffable goodness of God,
and his unutterable love for us. The more dearly a bridegroom

loves his bride, the longer he is wont to linger over the kisses
which he imprints on her lips, and the more ardently he knows
his love to be returned, the more closely does he press his lips
to hers.

Consider, then, the kiss of God, which has remained one un-
ceasing kiss ever since he touched the lips of flesh with the lips
of his Godhead, for having once assumed flesh he has never
laid it aside. Has he not pressed his mouth close to our mouths
in kissing us? So closely in very truth has he pressed it in this
kiss, that the one who kisses and the one kissed have thereby
become one, since the Word was made flesh that one who was
man might also be God, and one who was God also man.

O kiss, surpassing all other kisses in worth, full of sweetness
and deserving in return an embrace of most ardent love! However much men may kiss one another or love one another, they
still remain always numerically distinct, since they are two or
more separate individuals; but this is not so with the kiss of
our Lord's Incarnation, as we have said before. And, to speak
of how after kissing us he was to draw us into his body: there
are indeed other sacraments which are means of drawing us
into the mystical body of Christ, that is the Church, but the
sacrament by which we believe it is brought about was especially
set forth at the Last Supper, and he who instituted this same
sacrament speaks thus: 'He who eateth my flesh and drinketh
my blood abideth in me and I in him.'[287]

Or, if you prefer it, you can take Christ's two arms to be the
two Testaments, Old and New, with Christ's head in position
between them as the God of both, according to the apostle,
drawing unto himself the mysteries of each Testament, since he
is the mediator of both and the corner-stone which makes both
one.[288] But I myself do not think this any better, because he
did not show us the New Testament before he bestowed upon
us the kiss of the Incarnation.

Let this suffice for allegory, and now I should like to consider whether there is any moral fruit hidden within this sign,
and whether I can draw it forth into public view with the help
of our Lord Jesus Christ, of whom I am speaking.

(Ch. 44).   It often happens that those who have made a
careful study of the commentaries of learned men, and with

their help have been able to apply themselves without difficulty
to Sacred Scripture, understand the right hand to signify
prosperity and the left adversity in this world. Thus St Gregory,
explaining the meaning of Ezechiel's words: 'the face of a man
and the face of a lion at the right of all four, but the face of an
ox at their left',[288a] says: 'On our right we have joyful things
but on our left sad; hence we call what is unfavourable to us
"sinister".'[289] Relying on his authority I understand the right
hand to be the joy and prosperity with which the Lord cherishes
his chosen ones, lest they should succumb amidst tribulations;
the psalmist too supports me when he speaks thus to God:
'There are delights in thy right hand even unto the end', and
'thou hast given joy to me in tribulation'.[290]

The left hand I take to mean all the temporal misfortunes
with which the Lord chastizes his elect, so that, utterly aban-
doning the love of this world, they may hasten with all possible
speed to his embraces, whether the misfortunes which they
suffer consist in loss of temporal goods or in bodily infirmities.
For this reason it is written: 'Their infirmities were multiplied
and afterwards they made haste.'[291] Warned by such a sign,
then, God's elect draw nigh to the Lord, not by bodily steps
but by faith of heart which enlightens them, for, according to
the apostle, faith cleanses their hearts. Free from confusion
because of their hope, they hasten to the embraces of the
Saviour, for hope confoundeth not,[292] and by charity they
receive the kiss which the bride in the Canticle seeks when she
says: 'Let him kiss me with the kiss of his mouth.'[293]

What should we understand by the mouth of the Father but
the Son, and what by the kiss of the mouth but the Holy
Ghost? This kiss was solemnly imprinted on the mouth of
the Church when the Holy Ghost came down in tongues of
fire upon the Apostles, who may well be called the mouth
of the Church, for their sound has gone forth into all the
world and their words unto the uttermost ends of the earth.[294]
One of them, speaking of the bestowal of this kiss, says:
'The love of God is poured abroad in our hearts by the Holy
Spirit who is given to us',[295] and again: 'God hath sent the
Spirit of his Son into our hearts, crying: "Abba, Father"',[296]
and yet again: 'Whoever hath not the Spirit of Christ is none
of his.'[297]

(Ch. 45). According to the moral sense we are introduced into the body of Christ when we are confirmed in his love, and this is why John says in an epistle: 'God is love, and whosoever abideth in love, abideth in God.'[298] Hence too, Truth himself says: 'If anyone abide not in me, he will be cast out like a branch and will wither, and they will gather him up and cast him into the fire, and he burneth.'[299] This sentence should be a subject of great fear to those who do not love the Lord.

What does it mean that those who have fled to Christ, and been embraced, kissed and drawn into his body, are suckled by him, to follow up the order of the aforesaid metaphor, and what precious gift do they receive from him? If I wished to speak the exact truth, I should say plainly that I do not know how to answer this. For all that, however, I will by no means hold my peace on this account, but like a blind man I will now set myself to tapping at it with my stick.

To the question what they suck from him, I reply with the Scriptures: 'Honey from the rock'[300] and sweetness from Christ. Only those who have actually experienced the sweet savour of this rock know this sweetness, for it is a hidden manna, unknown to all who have not tasted it.[301] If the question is raised as to what precious gift they receive, I answer: that of which Truth speaks in the gospel: 'The kingdom of heaven is like unto a merchant seeking good pearls. Having found one pearl of great price, he went away and sold all that he possessed and bought it.'[302] This pearl is the gem which Christ gives to such as these. St Gregory says that this gem is 'heavenly desire, and if anyone has once had perfect knowledge, in so far as is possible, of the sweetness of this, he gladly leaves everything dear to him in this world'. And he adds: 'Compared with it all else seems worthless; he leaves his possessions, distributes what he has amassed, his heart on fire with desire for the things of heaven; nothing on earth pleases him now; any earthly thing in whose beauty he once took pleasure seems ugly, because the splendour of the pearl of great price alone shines in his mind.' And a little further on: 'Just as death kills the body, so love of eternal life slays love of transitory things, for,' he goes on to say, 'it renders anyone of whom it takes complete possession as it were insensible to earthly desires without'.[303] Undoubtedly this man has sucked honey from the rock, since he was able to address to us so many heartfelt words on the subject. But since I and those like me have received no such thing, we are weak and infirm in this part.[304]

That is enough for the tropological sense; it remains to examine the anagogical meaning. Though at first frightened by what is written: 'To whom has the arm of the Lord been revealed?'[305] afterwards I was encouraged on finding elsewhere: 'The Lord hath prepared his arm before the eyes of all nations.'[306] I shall not attempt to tell of his generation, but only, that the Lord may make known to me his salvation, how he has revealed his justice in the sight of the nations.[307]

(Ch. 46).   What can I understand anagogically by the arms of the Lord other than the interpretation of St Gregory commenting on the Gospel text: 'They saw a young man sitting at the right side',[307a] etc., where he both asks and at the same time answers a question of this sort: 'For what is signified by the left but this present life, and what by the right but eternal life?'[308] and he quotes in support the words of the Canticle: 'His left hand is beneath my head and his right hand will embrace me.'[309] On his authority I will now begin to comment for myself on this text; by the right hand of the Lord I understand the eternity of the life to come, by his left hand the riches and glory of this world, whence it is written: 'In his right hand is length of days and in his left riches and glory.'[310] And it is fitting that the bridegroom's left hand should be said to be beneath the bride's head, because the Church of the elect is enabled by means of it to transcend riches and earthly glory, despising them in her heart, and is also very soon prepared for the embrace of the right hand which is above.

In fact the mercy of our Redeemer is so great that he bestows merits on us with one hand, and with the other hand rewards us, for, according to Augustine: 'When God crowns our merits it is nothing else but his own gifts that he is crowning.'[311] O the ineffable goodness of God! Since he is just, it behoves him only to give rewards where there are merits, and because he is good, he does not wish to keep his riches for himself, so, finding nothing in us which he can reward but rather what should be punished, he gratuitously causes within us merits which he can afterwards juſtly reward. Thus the prophet addresses these words to God: 'Thou haſt wrought all our works in us.'[312] And the Apoſtle says: 'What haſt thou, O man, that thou haſt not received?'[313]

It is likewise not unfitting that I should take Chriſt's left hand to ſtand for the riches and glory of our heavenly home, as Scripture says: 'In his left hand are riches and glory';[314] and the psalmiſt, speaking of the latter, says appropriately: 'Glory and riches are in his house.'[315] Holiness becometh this house unto length of days,[316] and this is said to be in his right hand.

(Ch. 47). It is these arms, then, that will embrace the Church as represented by her triumphant members on high. But now we muſt consider the kiss to be beſtowed in that heavenly home. For this kiss signifies something great, nay, very great. The union of Chriſt with the Church, do you think? What is a kiss or what is kissing but the union of one person's mouth with another's? And what is this union but an expression of mutual love? So a kiss is a link or unbreakable seal, uniting two lovers together.

What else can I say this link is but the Holy Ghoſt, who, as we know, is the bond between the Father and the Son and the love of both of them, whence it is written: 'In the Father there abides eternity, in the Son equality, in the Holy Ghoſt the union of eternity and equality'?[317] No one can eſtablish another kiss or another bond between Chriſt and the Church than that which is aĉtually there, namely the Holy Spirit who transforms us into the self-same image after which we were made.[318] This he does through the influence of the Exemplar on the image; power influencing the memory, wisdom the intelleĉt and goodness or love the will, and thus the soul becomes deiform and like unto God amongſt the sons of God.[319] Thus he enables it to gaze with face unveiled upon the glory of God, as the Apoſtle says: 'We know that when he appears we shall be like to him, because we shall see him as he is.'[320] So much for the kiss. It remains for us to go into the queſtion of the gem which the Lord will show his eleĉt in heaven.

(Ch. 48). What else is a gem but some beautiful objeĉt which immediately delights the mind of the beholder, or at

least gives him cause for delight? I know of nothing else that
this gem can be save him whose beauty the sun and moon
admire,[321] and upon whom the angels desire to gaze.[322] He
bears witness to his Father and himself in the words: 'This is
eternal life, that they should know thee, the only God, and
Jesus Christ whom thou hast sent',[323] and again he says: 'Whoever loves me shall be loved by the Father and I will manifest
myself to him.'[324] Hence it is written: 'Eye hath not seen, O
God, besides thee what things thou hast prepared for them that
love thee',[325] and again: 'Eye hath not seen nor ear heard
neither hath it entered into the heart of man what things God
has prepared for them that love him.'[326]

Nothing then can be seen or imagined equal to this treasure;
though we have never beheld its beauty we believe it to be
great indeed, seeing that the Son of God chose to be crucified
in order to bring us to the vision of its loveliness. We must not
esteem lightly something for which so great a person chose to
suffer so much that we might gaze upon its beauty. To behold
this treasure just for one day would surpass all the riches and
glory of this world, even were a man to live for countless years,
enjoying all these things to his heart's content. St Augustine,
at the end of the third book of his work on free-will, speaks of
the same thing in these words: 'So great is the beauty of
divine justice and such the bliss of eternal light, that is to say
of immutable truth and wisdom, that even if it were only
granted one to remain with them for a day, it would be just
and reasonable on this account alone to despise the abundance
of this world's goods and countless years of this life, packed
with delights.'[327] So much for the precious gift.

(Ch. 49). We still have to ask what it is that those who are
embraced suck, and in what way those who receive the kiss
drink from Christ's breast. The answer is given by that amanu-
ensis of God and trusted mouth-piece of the Holy Ghost when
he says to God: 'They shall be inebriated with the abundance
of thy house, and thou shalt give them to drink of the torrent
of thy delight.'[328] And the wise man also says: 'The soul which
inebriates, shall itself be inebriated.'[329] This inebriation and
draught of delight are only known to those who experience

them; those who see God face to face, with whom is the source of life. It was this spring that the prophet was thirsting for when he said: 'My soul has thirsted for God, the living spring.'[330]

So much for what they drink from the breast of Christ; let us now see whether they are drawn thence into the body of Christ. The psalmist supports this idea when he says to the Lord: 'In thee is the dwelling as it were of all who rejoice.'[331] And Paul refers to the great sacrament of Christ and the Church the words that Adam spoke when he awoke from sleep, concerning himself and his wife. What words? The following: 'This is now bone of my bone and flesh of my flesh, for which cause a man shall leave father and mother and cleave to his wife, and they shall be two in one flesh',[332] and Truth, speaking to us all in the person of the apostles, has commanded us saying: 'Abide in me.'[333] If we abide in him we need have no fear of being cast out, because, as he himself said, he will not cast out anyone who comes to him; such a one shall abide for ever,[334] so that even in death he shall not be cut off but shall remain in our heavenly home, world without end. Amen.

(Ch. 50). I have spent some time in explaining the sign by means of which we may fly from before the bow, but now let me resume the course of my meditation, so as to speak to my Lord more freely. I will say to my Lord: 'There is safety for me in hastening to thine embrace, for thou art my refuge from besetting affliction, a helper in due time and in distress[335]; it is sweet indeed for me to receive the kiss of thy mouth, thou who hast committed no sin nor is guile found in thy mouth,[336] and it is the greatest delight to me to suck the breast of the king, who has been my hope from the bosom of my mother, and upon whom I was cast from the womb.'[337] But I also need to enter again into the womb of my Lord, and be reborn unto life eternal,[338] if I am to be amongst the members of the Church whose names are in the book of life.[339] For the Church must return thither whence she came forth, and to enter into her reward must be born again of him who first gave her birth that she might merit. For this reason the days on which the saints departed from this world to go to Christ are called their birthdays.

But who is worthy of such things? Certainly not I, since in exchange for the golden garment of the virtues I have embraced the dung of vile sins.[340] My right hand is the right hand of iniquity, my mouth defiled, my lips uncircumcized from my youth upwards,[341] and I am unworthy to have a share in the Saviour's fount, since I have nothing with which to draw, and the well is deep.[342] How dare I presume to enter into the tabernacle of God, in which the whole fullness of the Godhead dwells bodily,[343] when my nakedness is uncovered by reason of my impurity?[344]

(Ch. 51). What am I to say, Lord? Shall I say: 'Depart from me for I am a sinful man'?[345] God forbid! Rather let me say: 'because I am a sinful man draw nigh to me, and heal me, O my God, with the remedy of penance'.[346] For those who are well have no need of a physician, but those who are sick.[347] 'Depart' was the word of one who had not yet grasped the meaning of the Scriptures but was still without understanding; this is not surprising, seeing that the Spirit who was to teach him all things was not yet given, for Jesus was not yet glorified.[348] Similarly on another occasion, when Peter would have prevented our Saviour from undergoing death, he was told to go behind because he did not savour the things of God.[349] He certainly showed devotion in considering himself unworthy of being approached by our Lord, but it was not according to knowledge; for our Saviour penetrates everywhere on account of his purity, and even though he were to touch pitch he would not be defiled by it.[350]

So, precisely because I am a sinner, I have fled to thee; since there is nowhere I can flee from thee save to thee. Thou dost stretch out thine arms to receive me and bend down thy head to kiss me; thou dost bleed that I may have to drink, and open thy side in thy desire to draw me within.

What then shall separate me from the love of Christ,[351] and prevent me from casting myself into his embrace, when he stretches out his hands to me all day long?[351a] Shame at the sinfulness and impurity which defile me? No indeed; a shame that would separate me from my Lord would be fatal. I will rather run to him as he beckons me to come, and by touching him I shall be cleansed from all impurity of body and soul. Should I fail to do so I would hear the words of Wisdom reproaching me: 'I stretched out my hand and thou didst not look; thou hast despised all my advice, and I shall laugh at thy destruction.'[352] 'No, Lord, not so! I will gladly run to thee albeit a sinner, albeit unclean, for with thee there is merciful forgiveness; thou wilt wash me in thy blood, and I shall be made whiter than snow.[353] I will enter into thee and not stay without, for outside thee there is no salvation.'

I will speak to thy heart and say: 'Let me pitch my tent here, for I dare not remain outside on account of the wrath of the Lamb. Kind, humble heart, allow me to hide with thee from the face of the Lord's anger, for he is coming to judge the world! If thou choosest the left side, then let me remain on the right;[354] Christ's body is not so strait that it cannot hold us both at once. So let us make here two tabernacles, one for thee and one for me,[355] and there will still be room for Abraham, Isaac and Jacob to take their places, together with all those who have followed their way of life.' And the heart of Jesus answers me: 'If thou didst not desire to dwell with me, I would not have allowed thee to enter in here. But now, since it is my delight to dwell with the sons of men,[356] I will not cast out him that cometh to me.[357] Where I am, there let him be whom I love and by whom I am loved.'[358]

(Ch. 52). What fidelity, what goodness, what love! The safest possible fortress and refuge for those who are in anguish of mind! It is a fact that if a strong, valiant man happens to be holding some greatly treasured object at a moment when he suddenly sees a chance of avenging himself on his enemies, he immediately hides it in his bosom, and, snatching up a weapon, hurries off to the attack. So it is with our Lord, who is strong and mighty in battle, and in whose hand are the souls of the just which he loves most dearly; when that day comes of a sudden, that day of wrath, he will hide them in the secret place of his countenance,[359] until he has wrought vengeance upon his enemies.

That is why it is said that the dove in the clefts of the rock[360] is the Church in the wounds of Christ, for just as Eve came forth from the side of her husband, so the Church, Christ's bride, came forth when the water and blood flowed from his pierced side. Water represents people according to the words of the Apocalypse: 'the waters are the peoples',[361] and so the water flowing from Christ's side is the people of the Lord, the sheep of his pasture,[362] a holy nation, a purchased people, ransomed by the Lord.[363] This is the Church of the elect which the Lord hath redeemed from the hand of the enemy,[364] and like the rivers in Ecclesiastes which 'return to the place from whence they sprang to flow again',[365] she must go back whence she came forth.

Where, I ask, could there be a safer refuge than in Christ Jesus, our Lord, who rejects none that cometh to him, and never abandons what he has once taken up? No one can snatch anything out of his hand,[366] for he is the strong man armed, invincible and unperturbed,[367] who stands in awe of no one and pays heed to none out of fear.[368] Let us then cast ourselves and all our care upon him, for he has care of us.[369]

(Ch. 53).   Study then, O man, to know Christ: get to know your Saviour. His body, hanging on the cross, is a book, open for your perusal. The words of this book are Christ's actions, as well as his sufferings and passion,[370] for everything that he did serves for our instruction.[371] His wounds are the letters or characters, the five chief wounds being the five vowels and the others the consonants of your book. Learn how to read the lamentations and alas! too, the reproaches, outrages, insults and humiliations which are written therein.

However much else you may know, if you do not know this, I count all your learning for naught, because without knowledge of this book, both general and particular, it is impossible for you to be saved. So eat this book which in your mouth and understanding shall be sweet, but which shall make your belly bitter,[372] that is to say your memory, because he that increases knowledge increases sorrow too,[373] and hardship gives understanding to the hearing[374] of one who through his compassion with Christ crucified fills up in his flesh the sufferings which are wanting.[375]

There are many who know all sorts of things, such as the

natures of beings, the movements of the stars, the extent of periods of time, the measurements of places, and so forth, but because they are ignorant of this one thing, Jesus Christ and him crucified,[376] those other things profit them nothing unto their eternal salvation. May this book never depart from my hands, O Lord, but let the law of the Lord be ever in my mouth, that I may know what is acceptable in thy sight.[377]

(Ch. 54).   If I consider carefully the nature and number of the proofs of thy love which thou hast shown me from the first, it will be but a small return for such gratuitous love if I give thee my poor love in exchange according to the extent of my knowledge and capacity. When I ponder in my heart how much thou must have loved me, even before I was born, to choose to suffer death on the cross rather than to allow me to be separated from thee for ever, I see that complete self-surrender on my part is due to thee, and that thou hast deserved to be loved by me above all others in return. By many signs indeed thou dost confirm me in my hope that I am one of those for whom thou didst come to die,† and although no one can tell whether he be deserving of love or hate, I ought not to think otherwise than I have just said.

Whatever I have done from my youth thou hast turned to such good, O Lord, that it has, I believe, either caused me an increase of merit or made me more humble, thus being at once a warning against future sin and a punishment for that of the past, the greatest of all sins, pride. So thou didst cleanse me, O Lord, from the greatest sin when thou didst change my mourning into joy, when thou didst convert what I ought to have grieved over into an opportunity of acquiring humility, through which we find rest for our souls, and in which thou wilt give joy and gladness to my hearing.[378] Not only when things went well have I found thee a lover, O Lord, but I know thee also in a wonderful way as a most sure protector amidst evils. For I fell into frightful sins, and if thou hadst delivered me up unrepentant to death as I deserved, I should most justly

---

†The author's language here would not now be theologically accurate, for the Church has since declared against Jansenius that Christ died for all men and not only for the elect.

have been damned, if left to myself; but thou, as I say, when
according to the psalm thou wert judge, since against thee alone
I sinned and all judgement is given to the Son,[379] didst over-
look thy right for the time being as far as punishment was
concerned, and preferring instead to become my advocate, didst
avert the penalty and gratuitously restore me to a state of grace.

Thou, sweet Jesus, art all my good; thou art my ability in
work and eloquence in conversation, my proficiency in study,
and achievement in enterprise, my consolation in adversity
and caution in prosperity. Whichever way I turn, thy grace and
thy mercy go before me, and often when it seemed that all
was over with me, thou didst suddenly deliver me. Thou hast
brought me back when I went astray, instructed me in my
ignorance, corrected me in my sin, consoled me in sorrow and
comforted me in despair. When fallen thou didst raise me up,
when standing thou didst uphold me; on my going out thou
didst lead me, on my coming in receive me. When I consider
thy care for me, it truly seems to me, if I may so speak, that
thou hast naught else to do but to provide for my well-being,
and I see thee so completely taken up with looking after me,
that it is as if thou wert unmindful of all else and desirous of
attending to me alone.

(Ch. 55). O Lord of hosts, Jesus most lovable, what has
caused thee to be so solicitous in my regard that thou hast not
only willed that the heart of thy servant should experience that
delightful, hidden presence, which overflows with fullness of
joy and avails for love's closest embraces, not only chosen to
give me that hope which thou givest to other sons of the
Church through patience and the consolation of the Scriptures[380]; that would not suffice thee, but over and above it all
thou must needs teach me, not through thy beloved evangelist
John who proffered my petition to thee but with thine own
mouth, how I could be saved on the day of judgement; for that
was my petition. Merrily and with mild countenance thou didst
call out in reply: 'Love, and thou shalt be saved.'

This treasured visit of thine, O Lord, and thy salutary counsel do indeed compel me to love thee, but when I recall the

gaiety and kindness with which thou didst utter these words, then does gladness truly fill my heart. For thou didst speak as though thou wert laughing.

(Ch. 56). Help me then, Jesus, so to fulfil thy command that I may love thee in all things and above all things, Lord, in a measure which knoweth no measure,[381] and not in the way of those who, merely because they do not hate thee, say they love thee. I do not think that there is any creature who could find grounds for hating thee either within himself or in thee, although there is mention of such in sacred Scripture, as for instance: 'The pride of them that hate thee ever ascendeth',[382] and elsewhere: 'Them that hated thee, O Lord, have I not hated?'[383] And in another place Truth says: 'But now they have known and hated both me and my Father.'[384]

Here it should be explained that hatred can be understood in two different ways, either as a movement of the heart or else as manifested in act. With regard to the movement of the heart, no one hates God in his heart, if this is in accord with orthodox doctrine; but as regards the outward act many are said to hate God because they do things which God himself hates, such as committing sins of pride and manifest ingratitude. This is plainly shown in the above quotations, for when it says: 'The pride of them that hate thee ever ascendeth', it means: 'Such men are known to hate thee by the fact that their pride continues to increase.' And the same explanation is to be given to the other text: 'Them that hated thee' . . . and so on, for the psalmist first gives his reason for saying this in the words: 'Because you say in your thought: They will take the cities in vain',[385] as though he were to say: 'You are said to hate God because you proudly exalt yourselves before God in thought, believing that it is possible for some to take cities by human strength without the arm of the Lord.'

(Ch. 57). Now as for those words of my Lord's: 'They have hated me', etc. with the assistance of him who uttered them, I will attempt to explain them, if it please him. It was because of their ingratitude, O Lord, that thou didst complain of them in this way, for if thou hadst not come and spoken to them, they would not have had such a sin of ingratitude, and if thou hadst not wrought for them such works as no one else had done, they would not have had sin.[386] But now they have no excuse for their sin because they hated thee without cause, not indeed as God but as a man who was odious to them because thou didst reprove their works. This was evident when they agreed together that if anyone openly confessed thee to be the Christ, he should be expelled from the synagogue.[387]

No creature can hate God, and so Augustine, commenting on the Gospel text: 'either he will hate the one . . .', says: 'No one's heart can hate God',[388] and in his book of Retractations, with reference to the same passage, says: 'There are many of whom it is written: "The pride of them that hate thee ever ascendeth"' and goes on: 'No creature hates God in feeling, though he may in dealing', which is the same as saying: 'not according to the disposition of the will although it may be manifested by actions'.[389]

It seems to me a very wretched sort of love which springs not from any desire of the heart but merely from an absence of hatred. In the case of something which I never even think about, I cannot be said to love it just because I do not hate it. It is not love of that sort which the Lord has chosen, but such as he wrote with his finger for Moses on the summit of Mount Sinai, for him to teach to the children of Israel using these words: 'Thou shalt love the Lord thy God with thy whole heart and with thy whole soul and with all thy strength. This is the first and greatest commandment.'[390] Such is the love which I have chosen, saith the Lord.

(Ch. 58). Moreover anyone who declares that he loves God merely because he does not hate him, and yet does not keep this commandment, is a liar, for not even the devil himself hates him in so far as he knows him to be God but only in so far as he feels the punishment inflicted by him.[391] Let such a man hearken to our Lord's utterance: 'He that loveth me not keepeth not my words', and elsewhere: 'He that gathereth not with me scattereth, and he that is not with me against me',[392] that is to say on the devil's side, and this is not an indication of love but of hatred.

From my youth, O Lord, I have longed for this love which thou enjoinest, but I confess I have not as yet attained it, although I have besought thee for it in prayer. Nevertheless I will not cease from pleading until I receive it, for it has fallen to me to taste the first fruits thereof, and thou hast placed a sign on my face, that I should admit no lover but thee.[393] I am confident, O Lord, that thou wouldst not have given this pledge, if thou didst not intend to add what is still wanting. O that thou wouldst say to me with that same word by which thou didst make all things, thou whose very words are deeds: 'Take it by the tail!'[394] And even if thou delayest to do this, I will wait for thee, O Lord, until thou grant me thy salvation. Perfect, good Jesus, what thou hast wrought in me; I am indeed far from ungrateful for this small gift, only anxious for what is still lacking. What I ask for is exceeding great and sublime, and can only be reached by degrees.

(Ch. 59). For there are nine degrees of love which lead up to God, like Jacob's ladder reaching from earth to heaven. Three are comprised within the affections of the heart, three in the love of the soul, and three in the love of strength, that is of fortitude, as it is written: 'Thou shalt love the Lord thy God with thy whole heart', which refers to the affections, 'with thy whole soul', which refers to spiritual love, and 'with all thy strength', which refers to the steadfast love of choice.

St Bernard speaks to this effect in his twentieth sermon on the Canticle: 'Unless I come across a better interpretation of this threefold distinction I shall take it that love of the heart refers to a kind of enthusiastic affection, love of the soul to diligence or rational judgement, but love of strength to steadfastness and vigour of mind', and he likewise says: 'Affection is sweet, love prudent, the love of choice strong.'[395]

(Ch. 60). The first degree of affective love is when one is more drawn to the man Christ Jesus than to any other human being in the whole world, for the reason that such sublime Majesty chose to become man, and also because of all he then endured in the flesh. One can say with the Apostle: 'Whoever loveth not the Lord Jesus, let him be anathema',[396] and with the bride of the Canticle: 'My beloved is fair and ruddy, chosen out of thousands'[397]; he is comely in form beyond the sons of men; it is good for me to cleave to him and to rely on the support of such a man.[398]

He descended from heaven to earth and assumed flesh precisely that I might love him more than all others. Bernard affirms this in the same place in the following words:

> I believe that the chief reason why God, who is invisible, willed to be seen in the flesh and to converse with men as man, was that in the case of carnal men, who could not love save in a carnal way, he might first attract all their affections to a salutary love of his humanity, and so gradually lead them on to spiritual love.[399]

This affective love then is sweet, for I should say that it is indeed sweet that the Creator of man should have been and still be a man himself. Anyone who ponders on this fact will, I doubt not, straightway pronounce it sweet.

(Ch. 61). The second degree of affective love is when one delights in hearing nothing so much as what refers to Christ. Then one can truly say with the bride to the bridegroom: 'Let thy voice sound in my ears, for it giveth joy and happiness to my hearing.'[400] So it was that Peter would not go away and leave Christ because he had the words of eternal life,[401] referring to which Christ himself says: 'My sheep hear my voice',[402] and again: 'He that is of God heareth the words of God.'[403] But on the other hand the Lord complains of a certain people, saying through the prophet: 'My people have not heard my voice and Israel has not hearkened unto me',[404] and gives special praise to another people totally different from the former: 'A people that I did not know rendered service to me; in the hearing of the ear they have obeyed me.'[405]

St Bernard in the same sermon says of anyone who has ascended to this degree: 'Filled with that love which attracts the human heart more especially towards the humanity of Christ and towards all that Christ did or commanded in the flesh, he is easily moved to compunction by everything he hears in this regard', and he adds: 'There is nothing he would rather listen to, nothing he reads more attentively, nothing he thinks about more often, nothing more delightful for him to ponder on.'[406] This affective love is the more pleasing in that it presupposes the sweetness of love as its very condition. For no one takes pleasure in hearing favourable things said about someone he does not love. A man must first be loved, if it is to be a pleasure to hear him well spoken of.

(Ch. 62). The third degree of affective love is when Christ is loved with the whole heart, and when love for him has increased to such an extent as to be able to curb all a man's passions. Such a one can say with the prophet: 'He has sent fire from on high into my bones'[407] and has pierced my flesh with his fear, so that my heart and my flesh have rejoiced in the living God,[408] who has now claimed for himself all that is within me, according to the words of the Apostle: 'I live, now not I, but Christ liveth in me.'[409] According to the precept of the same Apostle, for love of his members my members are put to death, that is to say concupiscence, adultery, murder and such like.[410]

Who would deny the sweetness of that love of Christ's humanity which can crucify man's flesh with its vices and concupiscences?[411] Bernard in an exhortation in the same sermon concerning the sweetness of Christ's humanity says: 'Let the Lord Jesus be a sweet and pleasant antidote in thy heart against the allurements of fleshly living, which are indeed sweet in an evil way, so that the one sweetness may prevail over the other, just as one nail drives out another.' This he calls loving Christ with one's whole heart, as he goes on to say in the following words: 'Devotion of this sort is so great that the aforesaid sweetness takes possession of the whole heart, freeing it from love of everything carnal and from fleshly allurements', and forthwith adds: 'This is indeed loving with one's whole heart.' And then he says something which should be very carefully noted:

Otherwise, if I were to put some human relationship or natural pleasure before the humanity of my Lord, so that I should be less well able to put into practice what he taught by word and example in his mortal life, would it not be evident that I did not by any means love with my whole heart? My heart would be divided, and I would obviously be devoting only part of it to his humanity while turning the rest to what concerned myself.

He ends the whole passage by saying:

To sum up briefly; to love with one's whole heart is to disregard
for love of the sacred humanity all that is attractive whether in
one's own person or in that of others, including also the pride of
this world.[412]

Thus far his words. All then goes to prove what a very
sweet thing it is to love Christ in this way with one's
whole heart, but it remains for us now to seek a yet higher
way[413] in which, as I have already said, there are three degrees
of love, all of them within the compass of the soul.

(Ch. 63).   The first degree of this love is when anyone loves
Christ so much as to devote himself almost ceaselessly to seeking means to please him; such a one can say with the prophet:
'How I have loved thy law, O Lord! All day long it is the subject of my thought.'[414] Or, to put it more plainly, it is as though
he said: 'Consider how greatly I love thee, for thou knowest it
well, seeing that I do not cease pondering on thy law the whole
live-long day.' Such a man has progressed from flesh to spirit,
from affection to love, from sweetness to wisdom which resides
in the soul, according to the wise man: 'The soul of the just is
the seat of wisdom.'[415] Though at first he knew Christ according to the flesh, he does not do so now. Happy indeed is that
soul which so dwells upon the law of the Lord by day and
night,[416] that it first knows what is pleasing in his sight and
afterwards always does the things that are pleasing to him;[417]
thus meditating ever on the justifications of the Lord, in order
to please him to whom it has engaged itself.[418]

It is no wonder if such a soul soon begins to relish and have
insight into the things, of which it is ever mindful, concerning
God's commandments; they are a source of life to it, and its
constant remembrance of them is the reason why the Lord has
filled it with wisdom and understanding. The psalmist testifies
to this when he says: 'Thou hast made me wiser than all who
teach me by thy commandment, for it is with me for ever', by
which he means, in his mind; then he adds: 'I have understood
more than the ancients because I have sought thy commandments.'[419]

This then is the reason he gives for his relishing the things of the Lord. He does not say: 'Because I went to school, because I have been taught by learned men', but 'because I have sought thy commandments.'[420] And so it is indeed. For there is a certain knowledge and understanding of the holy Scriptures which our Lord promises to give to those who walk in the way of his commandments; Bernard indeed acquired it amongst beeches and oaks.[421] It is vain for those who teach the doctrines of men to seek the Lord outside this way without fulfilling his precepts. Rather might it be said of them: 'You shall seek me and shall not find me, and where I am you cannot come',[422] for you seek in the wrong way, since you do not keep my commandments; your heart is blinded and foolish; you know not where the Lord is, but grope at noon as though it were night.[423]

May the sons of Agar hear this, that is the sons of the bondwoman not of the free,[424] who seek after that wisdom which is of this world; the sons of Belial, who, puffed up with knowledge, are wont to despise simple, unlettered folk who are not so learned as they are. Let the meek hear it too, and rejoice[425] that there is a knowledge of holy Scripture which is to be learnt from the Holy Ghost and is manifested in good works. Often enough a layman has it while a cleric has not, a fisherman has it but a rhetorician knows naught of it, an old woman has acquired it but not a doctor of theology. Its name is love or charity, for according to Gregory: 'Love itself is knowledge'[426] —that is knowledge of the one towards whom the love is directed. The measure of your love is the measure of your knowledge; if you love greatly, you know a great deal. Take the case of a very learned man who does not love God. What does he know about God? Let him answer that himself, and be ashamed in future to despise others. He may see their faces, but he does not see their hearts, in which a precious treasure may lie hidden, namely that very unction which would teach him all things,[427] and without which the wisdom of the wise is vain and the intelligence of the prudent is rejected by the Lord.[428] This unction is rightly believed to be the Holy Ghost, as it says in the hymn addressed to him by the Church:

> The Paraclete is thy blest name,
> Thou gracious gift of God most high;
> Thou living fount, pure fire, love's flame,
> And unction souls to fortify.[429]

God the Son also spoke of him to the apostles in these words: 'The Holy Ghost will bring to your mind whatsoever I have said to you.'[430]

(Ch. 64). Led by him a man is able to advance from what is carnal to what is spiritual, and taught by him is raised from sweetness of the flesh to wisdom of the spirit; and yet without his aid Christ cannot be loved even in his humanity, for this is a wholesome kind of affection, which leads not to death but to everlasting life. Our Lord showed sympathy when the apostles displayed such affection and did not reprove them when, before his Ascension, they were saddened at the prospect of the withdrawal of his bodily presence, and asked one another: 'What is this that he says, "a little while"? We do not know what he is saying.' He prudently restrained them with the following words: 'Because I have spoken these things to you, sorrow has filled your heart. But I tell you the truth: it is expedient for you that I should go, for if I do not go, the Paraclete will not come.'[431]

See how tactfully our Lord led his disciples from affection for his humanity to love of the Spirit; first of all he disclosed their sadness, and, condescending to their weakness, said these words: 'Because I have spoken, etc. . . .'; after that, emphasizing the truth of what he said, he gave them salutary advice: 'But I tell you . . .', and then explaining what would prevent the coming of the Spirit, he both gave them a warning and promised a gift: 'If I do not . . .', and immediately afterwards: 'When I shall have been taken up, I shall send him to you.'

(Ch. 65). Indeed this wise Master had gradually to win over his disciples' minds to consenting; bound as he was to them by the bonds of love, he did not wish to ascend without their consent. And so before his Ascension he said many things to them as if he would get them to agree, and, in a way, begged their permission to ascend, as for example: 'I go to him that sent me, and none of you asketh me: whither goest thou?'[432] It was as if he had said: 'How is it that you do not ask where I mean to go to, since you know my intention of ascending to

the Father, and I do not want to do so without your consent?'
Elsewhere he says: 'If you loved me, you would indeed be glad
because I go to the Father.'⁴³³ What! Did they not love him,
they who could not bear to hear a single word about his
departure? Had he himself not borne witness to them saying:
'For the Father himself loveth you because you have loved
me'?⁴³³ᵃ However, according to Bernard, 'they loved in one
way, and yet they did not love; they loved with sweetness
rather than with prudence, they loved according to the flesh
but not according to reason, in short they loved with their
whole heart but not with their whole soul'.⁴³⁴ That is how he
puts it.

(Ch. 66). For the love of God, dear reader, consider how
sweet must have been the companionship of him from whom
they could not bear to be separated save with great grief and
sorrow, and who spoke thus to them: 'Amen I say unto you,
you shall lament and weep while the world shall rejoice but
your sorrow shall be turned into joy.'⁴³⁵

It is said that after our Lord's Ascension Peter always carried
a kerchief in his bosom to wipe away the tears that would often
flow, for whenever he recalled our Lord's dear presence and
manner of speaking, he could not refrain from weeping for
excessive sweetness of love.⁴³⁶

(Ch. 67). The second degree of this love is when love of
God has increased to such an extent in any man that he rejoices
to do whatever he knows will be pleasing to Christ; love of this
sort is more prudent, since to good will it adds deeds. True
love effects great things, for as St Gregory says: 'Love that is
truly love is never idle.'⁴³⁷ On the other hand one who knows
what is right and does not do it is guilty of sin, and the servant
who knows the will of his lord and does not act accordingly
will be beaten with many stripes.⁴³⁸

The apostle shows the value of cheerfulness in well-doing
when he says: 'Each one according as he has determined in his
heart, not with sadness or of necessity,' and he adds: 'For God
loveth a cheerful giver.'⁴³⁹ See what cheerfulness wins for the

worker, the love of God himself. Nor is this surprising, for just as action is the proof of human love, so cheerfulness in the doer is a sign of the love of God. It was not for nothing that Paul, speaking of him that giveth, immediately added: 'with cheerfulness.'[440]

(Ch. 68). I am therefore of the opinion that cheerfulness adds just as much to an action as action adds to right intention, for cheerfulness in the doer is at once both a sign and an effect of a loving heart, and if we have not got that, all we do goes awry. As Gregory says: 'Charity alone makes what is done enduring, and nothing deserves the name of a good action if it does not spring from the root of love';[441] and so the Wise Man says: 'Son, in all that thou dost, show a cheerful countenance.'[442] Even amongst men it is always a cause of displeasure if anything is given with a gloomy face or a task performed with murmuring; how much less acceptable then in the eyes of God is that which is not done gladly or with goodwill? There is certainly nothing more precious than goodwill, and so the Church sings of our most blessed patron Cuthbert:

> Rejoicing he did e'er fulfil
>   The law of God throughout his days,
> With bounteous, radiant, gay goodwill;
>   His merits won him lasting praise.[443]

(Ch. 69). For a cheerful countenance springs from a joyful heart and the security of a good conscience,[444] hence Solomon says in Proverbs: 'A joyful heart cheereth the countenance, and a sad spirit drieth up the bones',[445] and again: 'A tranquil mind is like a continual feast.'[446] And so holy men, the elect of God, are wont to be joyful and show a cheerful face even in trying circumstances, thanks to their sincere examination of conscience before God and to the fervour of divine love towards God and their neighbour which burns within them.[447] So Paul says: 'For this is our glory, the testimony of our conscience.'[448]

"SS John the Baptist and John the Evangelist" from MS Douce 231 Fol 2R, from A Book of Hours, *Sarum Use, early 14th Century, English.*

"Assumption with Angels" MS Douce 79 Fol 3R, fragments from a Passion of Christ and Other Texts, *English early 14th Century.*

"King David playing the Harp", MS Douce 366 Fol 10R, The Ormsby Psalter, *East Anglian c. 1300.*

"Coronation of the Virgin" MS Douce 79 Fol 3V, fragments from A Passion of Christ and Other Texts, *English early 14th Century.*

In the book which Bede wrote on the life and miracles of the most blessed Cuthbert, our incorrupt patron, he said of him:

> He was a man outstanding in the virtue of patience, and absolutely indomitable in bearing courageously whatever sufferings of mind or body afflicted him. His face was no less cheerful in times of sadness, so that it was obvious that he was inwardly consoled by the Holy Ghost, and so despised outward tribulation.[449]

The Wise Man says: 'The just man will not be saddened, no matter what befall him';[450] this we must understand as meaning 'by the passion of sadness'; though perhaps he will be superficially affected. It is to this I take these other words of David to refer: 'If the just man falleth he shall not be bruised.'[451] It is as if he said: 'Although the just man may be superficially saddened in adverse circumstances, since no one can resist first movements, yet he will not be overcome by the passion of sadness, that is he will not be altogether thrown off his balance, since no one can separate such a man's inner self from the love of Christ.' According to Paul:

> Neither tribulation nor distress nor persecution nor hunger nor nakedness nor danger nor the sword, neither death nor life, neither angels nor archangels, neither principalities nor powers, neither things present nor things to come, neither might nor height nor depth, nor any other creature shall be able to separate us from the love of God which is in Christ Jesus our Lord.[452]

Happy indeed is that soul which, thanks to the testimony of its own conscience, can say to the Lord with the prophet: 'My portion, O Lord, I have said is to keep thy law';[453] in other words: 'I said that for the future it would be my portion to have strength to keep thy law.' To such a soul all the Lord's commands have become more desirable than gold and many precious stones, sweeter than honey and honey-comb,[454] and because of the greatness of its love they seem to it but little.[455] If the Lord bids it keep his commandments with exceeding care, it can answer forthwith that it is ready and not troubled about doing so, since it has now come to love them more than gold and topaz, and rejoices at his words like one who finds abundant spoils.[456]

4

(Ch. 70). The third degree is reached when a man is so fired with the love of God that he is neither elated by prosperity not cast down by adversity, and if riches abound, he by no means sets his heart on them;[457] if he happen to lose them, it causes him no regret at all.

This is the wisest and most perfect love of God and is itself proof that all worldly love is dead. For who can be wiser than the man who has lost all taste for this world and delights in the love of God alone, whose heart is so possessed by divine love that there is no place within him where God is not loved? Attachment to temporal goods distracts the mind from love of divine things, and it is evident that the more intense delight a man takes in the things of this world, the less he loves God. And so St Gregory in his thirtieth homily on the Gospel commenting on the text: 'If anyone love me',[457a] says: 'The delight a man takes in things below is the measure of his distance from celestial love.'[458] Concerning this same matter Truth himself says: 'No one can serve two masters.'[459] The Venerable Bede explains this as follows: 'No one can serve two masters, because no one can love at the same time both things transitory and things eternal. For if we love eternity, we make use of all temporal things without becoming attached to them.'[460] That is Bede's view. St Gregory also speaks of this degree of perfection in his fifth homily on the Gospel, when, commenting on the passage: ' Jesus walking',[460a] he says: 'This sacrifice is not completely made unless the desires of this world are entirely abandoned', and what he says next should be very carefully noted: 'For the desire of anything earthly here below is quite certain to give rise within us to envy of our neighbour.'[461]

(Ch. 71). What then, I ask, is the nature of charity? Let those attend who flatter themselves that they are holy while they yet greatly covet earthly things and, full of ambition, pursue the honours of this fleeting world; those who, though their tonsure marks them as liars,[462] seem to be able to say to the Lord: 'Behold we have left all things and have followed thee.'[463] They have not really done so, for their hearts are still attached to the things which their habit proclaims them to have abandoned, and in their avarice they fly from him whom they

have oftensibly made profession of following in the way of
love. He who is the Truth shows up men of that sort to us, and
at the same time teaches us to be on our guard againft them.
He also gives us a sign whereby they can plainly be recognized:
'Beware of false prophets', he says, 'who come to you in the
clothing of sheep, inwardly however they are ravening wolves;
by their fruits you shall know them.'⁴⁶⁴ Such men neither despise earthly things nor follow the Lord, for they seek the things
of this world, and though they honour God with their lips
their heart is far from him.⁴⁶⁵ The Church might well apply to
them the words: 'Behold in peace is my bitterness moſt
bitter.'⁴⁶⁶ That is to say: 'See how I am moſt bitterly afflicted
by those whom I am supposed to possess in great peace.'

So too the bride in the Canticle, speaking in the name of the
Church, utters this complaint: 'The sons of my mother have
fought againſt me.'⁴⁶⁷ They are rightly called sons of her
mother, not of her father, because although they seem to be in
the Church as sons, nevertheless their father is the devil, and
they will be condemned with him at the judgement.

St Augustine says of such men: 'Juſt as I know none better
than those who have gone forward in the religious life, so I
know none worse than those who have made a failure of it.'⁴⁶⁸
And St Gregory in one of his homilies says: 'I do not think
that anyone in God's Church does more harm than the man
who wears a religious habit, and, though behaving unworthily,
enjoys a reputation for sanctity.'⁴⁶⁹

(Ch. 72).   Such as these are far removed from that degree of
love which enables anyone who has attained to it truly to say
with Paul: 'I know how to abound and how to suffer want.'⁴⁷⁰
I know how to abound, because the Lord is my portion, and
compared with him I reckon riches as naught. If they abound,
I set not my heart upon them, because where my treasure is,
there is my heart also⁴⁷¹; and I know how to suffer want, being
confident that nothing is lacking to those who fear God or love
him in truth.⁴⁷² If riches fail, I do not regret them, because
what is possessed without attachment is loſt without grief.
Such a one can say to the Lord with the prophet: 'For what
have I in heaven, and apart from thee what do I desire upon
earth?'⁴⁷³

I believe that Blessed Edmund, Archbishop of Canterbury, reached this degree. It is said that when Holy Viaticum was brought to him before he died he uttered these words: 'It is thou, O Lord, in whom I have believed, whom I have preached, concerning whom I have taught, and thou art my witness that during my sojourn on earth I have sought nothing but thee.'[474] In very truth he loved with his whole soul the Lord of whom he thus spoke, and he might well have said with the apostle: 'Our conversation is in heaven',[475] since it is St Augustine's opinion that the soul is more truly with the object which it loves than in the body which it quickens.[476]

(Ch. 73). The first degree of loving with one's strength is when the soul is so enkindled with ardent love, and one's motives so wonderfully and easily controlled by it, that whatever one thinks or does, is thought or done with a view to pleasing him who is loved so exceedingly: and love of this sort is strong. Anyone who has risen to this degree is on terms of intimacy with the Bridegroom, and often enjoys his embraces.

This is certainly food for the strong and not suitable for those who are as yet babes in Christ. I take it that the apostle was thinking of it when he said: 'I could not speak to you as to spiritual men but as to carnal', then he adds: 'I gave you not food but milk to drink, as though you were babes in Christ',[477] and elsewhere he says: 'We speak wisdom amongst the perfect.'[478] What wisdom is that? Surely that which he speaks of in another place when he says: 'I show you a yet higher way; if I speak with the tongues of men and angels but have not charity, I am nothing.'[479]

Since, however, charity may be taken to mean many different things according as it is used in a general, specific or particular sense, we must first consider the various definitions and then apply whatever has bearing on these points to the question under discussion.

(Ch. 74). Charity in the widest sense, according to the Master of the Sentences, is that love of God and one's neighbour by which God is loved for his own sake and our neighbour for God's sake, or, in other words, in God.[480] The whole law and the prophets depend upon this twofold charity,[481] which, in addition to the love which a man has for the humanity of Christ, also includes that which he has for the person of his neighbour and for his own body. As a result of this, first, according to our Lord's command, if he sees anyone naked he covers him and does not despise his own flesh,[482] and secondly, he flees from death and nourishes his body, for no one hateth his own flesh.[483]

Properly speaking, however, charity is love which always tends towards another. Hence St Gregory declares in his seventeenth Homily: 'Charity cannot exist where there are not at least two people. No one', so he says, 'can properly speaking have charity towards himself; love must be directed towards another if it is truly to be charity.'[484] This definition includes all meritorious love, both loving with one's soul and with one's strength, and this is a created virtue.

In a still more particular sense, however, according to John's epistle: 'God is charity.'[485] Hence also St Gregory, speaking in the same tenor, says: 'The Holy Ghost is love',[486] and Hugh in his treatise on the love of God affirms that: 'Charity alone enjoys the privilege of both being called and being God.'[487]

(Ch. 75). It is the second definition which applies to our present subject, and in that particular sense charity is love tending from one towards another, by which a man loves God with his whole strength according to the superior part of his reason. Augustine in Book 12 of his work on the Trinity asserts that it is 'reckoned part of the wisdom by which we contemplate things divine',[488] and I have reason for understanding thereby that wisdom which Paul 'spoke among the wise'.[489] He had experience of this degree of love and perfection and said: 'We know that to those who love God all things work together for their good.'[490] That is to say that whatever a man does or thinks, if he really loves God it is turned to his own good by him whom he thus loves. And so Augustine in his commentary on John's epistle says: 'Love, and do what you will',[491] as though he were to say: 'I tell you to do what you like, only on the understanding that you really love God, for no evil can proceed from a heart wholly possessed by genuine love of God.' The truth of this can be proved both by argument and the support of authority.

(Ch. 76).   Reason tells us that a man possessed of freedom does only what he chooses to do; but where there is love of God, there too is the Holy Spirit, and where the Spirit of the Lord is, there is freedom;[492] therefore whoever loves God possesses freedom. Whoever fulfils the law is no longer subject to it, especially as the law was not imposed on righteous men but was given for the sake of sinners. Whoever loves fulfils the law,[493] and so the just man is free to do what he will because he desires no evil. I shall now go on to prove this.

When anyone loves God with his whole heart and his whole soul, and has risen to the first degree of that love whereby God is loved with one's whole strength, then love has already taken complete possession of his will. But all the actions of a free man proceed from his will, and so those of one who loves in this way spring from charity; hence because of the greatness of his love, such a man's will might more truly be said to be charity than will.

We have the authority of Truth for thinking this, for he says: 'If thy eye is simple, thy whole body shall be full of light.'[494] Bede explains these words as follows: 'The body means our actions, the eye the inward intention from which they proceed, the quality of which determines whether they be deeds of light or darkness.' And he adds: 'If you try to perform what good deeds you can with a pure and unswerving intention, the works which you do will assuredly be works of light, even though in the eyes of men they may seem to have some imperfection about them.'[495]

(Ch. 77).   If, however, it is objected that there are certain actions which are wrong in themselves, such as adultery, murder, perjury and such-like, which are always sinful, the answer is that anyone who loves God to this extent neither wishes to do such things nor does them, especially since a will given up to such behaviour can never exist alongside charity, which, as Paul teſtifies, neither aĉts perversely nor thinks **any** evil.[496] Moreover he was inviting men to this degree of love when he said: 'Do all things to the glory of God,'[497] meaning, 'I would have you so full of love that whatever you do will turn out to be for the glory of God.' He foresaw that there would be devotion of this sort in the hearts of some, when he said: 'Pray without ceasing, giving thanks in all things',[498] as though to say: 'See that your thoughts and works are such that they will never cease to intercede with God on your behalf', as it is written: Hide your alms in the lap of the poor man, and they will pray to God for you.[499]

(Ch. 78).   For the love of God, dear reader, consider how precious to him that man muſt be who orders his thoughts and aĉtions with a view to pleasing the Lord continually in all of them, and who can truly say to him: 'Behold, I place thee as a seal upon my heart, submitting to thy good pleasure whatever I think in my heart, and as a seal upon my arm, since whatever I do is done to please thee.'[500] Should you ask whether a man of this sort commits sins, my answer would be: there is not a juſt man on the face of the earth doing good, who does not commit at leaſt venial sins, but these are as swiftly extinguished in the furnace of such charity as are the drops of water which a smith caſts into the midſt of the fire to make it burn more fiercely.

There may be another reason too why whatever a man in this ſtate thinks or does turns out to be meritorious and pleasing to the Lord: namely, love of this kind is so ſtrong that by virtue of it a man's aĉtions please him towards whom they are all direĉted. Such a lover has been endowed with grace, so that he may never again displease his Beloved. Before he conferred such grace upon him the Beloved foresaw all that the lover would do, and in spite of it gave him such grace that henceforth the Lord would never have cause to be wrath with him, nor would he perish from the way of juſtice.[501]

(Ch. 79).   The second degree of this love is when a man is on fire with the love of God to such an extent that excessive love causes him to be weary of life and to long for death. For him, as for Paul, to live is Christ and to die is gain,[502] and, since he cannot yet behold him whom his soul so greatly loves, he sinks down upon the bed of holy languor, so that in him is realized what is written 'Stay me up with flowers, compass me about with apples, for I languish with love',[503] and a little further on 'I adjure you, O daughters of Jerusalem, if you find my beloved, that you tell him that I languish with love',[504] and again 'In my bed by night I sought him whom my soul loveth.'[505]

It is a fact that at this degree love-sickness sweetly torments the lover, because he is withheld from the embraces of him whose delectable presence he has often enjoyed. Anyone who has advanced to this degree is already on terms of friendship with the bridegroom, who not only frequently lavishes his embraces upon him but even bestows upon him the holy delight of that ineffable kiss for which the bride in the Canticle eagerly begs when she says: 'Let him kiss me with the kiss of his mouth.'[506]

Bernard, commenting on the words of the Canticle: 'Stay me up with flowers', etc. says: 'The loss of a loved object increases your desire for it, and the more ardent the desire, the more grievous the loss.'[507] Solomon too speaks of this love-sickness: 'Hope deferred afflicts the soul',[508] and the man who uttered these words: 'I desire to be dissolved and to be with Christ'[509] was languishing with this love, as also when he said: 'Who shall deliver me from the body of this death?'[510]

(Ch. 80). O Apostle, dear unto God, why is your spirit so troubled, since you know whom you have believed, and are certain that he, a just judge, is able to keep what you have entrusted to him until that day?[511] Surely it is because the measure of love is to have no measure, and it will not submit to reason until that which is perfect be more fully bestowed and that which you have in part be done away.[512] You will not be rid of this complaint until you see Christ face to face, and know even as you are known.[513] You were referring to that when you said: 'I am even now about to be taken away, and the time of my release is at hand.'[514] When that moment came, O beloved of God, and you suffered martyrdom for love of him, the Lord filled your desire with good things.[515]

This is that enviable state in which the soul, languishing for love of the bridegroom, is like a mournful turtle-dove, which, having lost its mate, will never again as long as it lives perch on a green bough. Well might such a soul say: 'The voice of the turtle is heard in our land',[516] for it learnt from it this loving lament, when bodily strength gave way under such a weight of charity. Bernard comments on this passage in his 59th Sermon on the Canticle of Canticles, where he says: 'When some holy soul sighs for the presence of Christ, grieves at any delay in the coming of his kingdom, and groaning and sighing salutes its longed for home from afar, do you not think that in behaving like this on earth that soul is acting like the chaste and mournful dove?' He also applies it to himself in these words: 'Should not Christ's absence move me frequently to tears and daily make me groan?' Further on he reaffirms this: 'O Lord, all my desire is before thee and my groaning is not hidden from thee; I have laboured amidst my groans, thou knowest.[517] Not I alone, but all who love thy coming, have experienced this groaning.'[518] Here the quotation ends.

(Ch. 81). It is, however, worth noting that no one who arrives at this degree lives for long, and so it was that this very saint never finished his commentary on the Canticle, for when he was just explaining the meaning of the opening words of Chapter 3: 'In my bed by night I sought him whom my soul loveth', he died. I believe that this happened by divine dispensation so that we might understand from those ardent words of the bride's how outstanding was his merit and love for the bridegroom, seeing that just as he was commenting on the bride's bed and her longing, he took to his own bed, stricken down with fatal illness. From this we may reasonably conclude that the very passage he was explaining, 'In my bed', etc. can be applied in all truth to Bernard himself. Since, however, he understands these words to refer to consummate perfection, I will keep what he says for the third degree of this kind of love, which is the ninth altogether, where we will be considering the height of perfection.

I shall add but little about the degree which I referred to as the second, in order that I may pass on to the third. Since, however, I have had no experience of this degree, what can I say about it, save how blessed and happy is the soul to whom it is given to taste the delights which belong to it? As a certain poet says:

> Thy steadfast love affects me till
> I languish, Jesus, with love's ill;
> Thou fruit of life which ever will
> Sweet nectar for love's thirst distil.[519]

This is stronger than other love for it does not fail. Taking free will into account I admit that one who has such love might sin, but he does not sin; he might do wrong, but he does not.[520]

(Ch. 82).   The third degree of this kind of love, and the last and highest of all, is when a man is so much absorbed by the love of God and inebriated with it that he forgets himself, and does not know what he is doing apart from loving. He does not notice what he sees, nor understand what he hears; he does not realize what he is tasting, nor distinguish smells; he is unaware of what he is touching, because the surpassing delight of divine love within his heart makes him forget to use his five senses and his reason. So it is that to the world he seems a fool, and, being filled with the Holy Spirit, is deemed sodden with new wine.[521] Love of this sort so dilates the lover's heart that he cannot bear it any longer, and dies as the result.

This, then, is the most powerful kind of love, and it perfects loving with the whole strength through the intervention of death, which results when a soul which has advanced to this love of strength reaches its fullest capacity. As Augustine says in his book on the Perfection of Justice: 'No one can attain to such perfection in this life',[522] and St Bernard in his treatise on the Love of God says: 'I do not think that the command: "Thou shalt love the Lord thy God . . ." will be perfectly fulfilled until the heart is no longer obliged to take thought for its body and soul in this present state, or to concern itself with the protestations of the life of the senses.'[523]

So death must intervene if a man is to love God with his whole strength, and in fact it often does result from intense love. We read in the Canticle of Canticles: 'Love is strong as death.'[524] This has been shown to be literally true in the case of many, not only of those who have been struck down by the intensity of divine love, but I have even heard of many who have succumbed to an excess of blind passion, which in the case of an adult always leads to remorse of conscience. Because love diminishes where there is remorse in the lover's conscience, it follows that even when love of this kind is not so violent, it still cannot be whole-hearted love, since it is accompanied by fear of punishment.

It is quite the opposite with love of God, for the more he is loved, the more conscience is at peace, and the more conscience is at peace, the more intensely is the heart enabled to love. If, then, the strength of blind passion is great enough to slay the lover without fear of reprisal, how much more divine love? What love, save love for God, could completely put an end to a man's life? Or would you deny that love of God is able to do as much in man as nature can in a bird? I came across the following verses on the nightingale.

(Ch. 83). We read of this bird that when it feels its death approaching, it flies up into a tree very early in the morning and, raising its beak, pours forth its whole being in varied song.

Warbling beauteous melodies, it forestalls the morning,
But around the hour of Prime, just as day is dawning,
Louder grow the piercing strains of its tuneful warning;
So it sings without a break, pause or respite scorning.

When the hour of Terce has come, then it knows no measure,
For its heart expands still more with a songster's pleasure;
So as though its throat would burst—ne'er a moment's leisure—
Yet more ardently it spends all its vocal treasure.

When at noon the midday sun violently is blazing,
Then at length its small frame breaks with excess of praising,
And its wonted plaint anon 'turi-turi' raising,
Worn with song it faints away, seized with stupor dazing.

So the nightingale's life ebbs, with its body's breaking,
Till at last its beak alone trembles mutely shaking;
Should it live till None, it dies then beyond all waking,
Blood has left its riven veins, from it all life taking.

(Ch. 84). That is the natural behaviour of this bird and it has a most lovely significance, representing as it does the attitude of a devout soul to God. As it meditates on our Saviour's life and Passion throughout the successive periods of its life, the soul is at last so completely conformed to Christ that it dies from sheer excess of love. The author of the above lines declared that this is an actual possibility when he says of this degree of love:

> In this state is now renounced all that this world prizes;
> Earthly ease but poison seems which the soul despises.
> Mortal life when None is come sinks and no more rises,
> Love, in rending bonds of flesh, full force exercises.[525]

That is his testimony.

In the book of Psalms also the prophet says in the person of one dying in this way: 'My heart and my flesh have fainted away.'[526] I take 'heart' there to mean 'soul', according to what he says in another psalm: 'Who fashioned their hearts separately.'[527] The gloss says: 'that is, God creates souls individually and infuses them into the already developing bodies of the little ones'. I take 'flesh' to mean 'body', as the same prophet says: 'My heart and my flesh have rejoiced in the living God',[528] and that is, according to the commentary, 'My soul and my body.' But why did he say above: 'My heart has fainted away', and then immediately add as a reason: 'God of my heart, God is my portion for ever'? Surely it was as though he were to say: 'Since God has wished to be called the God of my heart, it is no wonder that my heart has fainted away for very love, for if the Lord is anyone's portion even in this life, his heart and flesh will soon say: "Lord, we have fainted away."'

(Ch. 85). No one ought to have difficulty in believing in such perfection, since it has been demonstrated by argument, supported by quotations, typified in the natural behaviour of birds, and will now be proved by an example.

There was once a very holy solitary who, amongst the other prayers which he unremittingly poured forth to God, begged him especially to reveal to him who would receive in Heaven reward like unto his own. God granted his prayer, and at an opportune time sent this message to him by an angel: 'In such and such a province there is a village where the lord of the manor is a knight, who has a daughter equal to you in merits; she will receive the same reward as you in heaven.' The hermit was told the name of both the place and the knight, as well as of the girl herself. He was, as may well be imagined, greatly cheered by this heavenly disclosure and, having set his cell and possessions in order, ſtarted off to find the place where the knight lived. When he got there, he was put up for the night in the village. He cross-queſtioned his hoſt minutely as to the manner of life of the knight and his lady, but he especially asked about the girl, on whose account he had come. Amongſt other things he at laſt ascertained from him that the knight's daughter was very merry, had a ſmiling countenance, and, as far as could be seen, did not appear particularly holy, except that she had preserved her virginity intaƈt, and had never been troubled by any suspicions with regard to her purity and good living. Having made these inveſtigations the hermit sent for the knight next morning, and asked him and the girl's mother if he might speak to their daughter and discuss things with her. This was granted him very readily, since his great reputation for sanƈtity had spread far and wide, and no one would think ill of him even if he did converse with a maiden.

Briefly this is what happened. The girl was summoned and the hermit queſtioned her about her manner of life; what, for example, she did in the way of praƈtising abſtinence, how rough her clothes were, how much she prayed, kept vigil, gave alms and so on. In answer to all these queſtions she claimed to do no more than other Chriſtians who lived an ordinary life. But as he queſtioned the girl ſtill more closely and told her the whole ſtory of the message which had brought him to such a remote region, she thereupon declared that she was of no great worth herself; all that she could say was that she loved Chriſt so much that she was nearly beside herself with joy when she heard the name of Jesus pronounced. 'And', she added, 'all the laughter and gaiety which make people think me frivolous arise from joy caused by the exceeding great love which I have for Jesus, my spouse, whom I love above all things, to whom my virginity is pledged, and to whom I have dedicated myself with complete devotion,[529] for he is my spouse, and I am his

bride.' The hermit was amazed at her words, and asked her in
astonishment whether she really did love Christ as much as she
said. 'Indeed I do', the girl replied, and so saying fell to the
ground and breathed her last in the hermit's arms. On seeing
this, her parents ran to the spot and, overcome with grief, tried
to find out from the man of God what had happened to their
daughter. He told them all that had taken place, and how it was
as the result of her ardent love for Christ that she had collapsed
and died in this way. When the parents heard this, they were
filled with great joy at the holiness of their child, and so their
grief was somewhat mitigated. She was buried, a glorious
martyr to the love of Christ, and afterwards the hermit returned
home rejoicing. Though he had previously thought of himself
as deserving little, now he praised God that a like reward was
in store for him.

(Ch. 86).　　Those incredulous people who, imagining themselves to be perfect, cannot believe that others are better than
themselves, should be convinced by this, especially since St
Gregory says that: 'Whoever has tasted the sweetness of
heavenly life as fully as is possible gladly leaves all that he
hitherto loved on earth', and a little further on: 'When love of
eternal life takes full possession of a man, it renders him immune
from earthly desires.'[530] Thus St Bernard in his eighty-ninth
sermon on the Canticle addressed love in these words:

> O love, you are indeed rash, violent, fragrant, impetuous, and
> brooking consideration of naught but yourself, you eschew all
> else and despise everything, content with yourself alone. You
> subvert order, disregard custom, recognize no measure. All that
> propriety, reason, self-respect, deliberation and judgement would
> seem to demand you triumph over, and reduce to captivity within
> your grasp.[531]

It should be clear enough to all that a passion which recognizes no measure will not hesitate to slay when it is confronted
by death. Otherwise, if it acknowledged death as a limit and
took care to keep out of its way, it would be recognizing some
measure, which would be a contradiction in terms. That the
opposite is true is shown by the martyrs, whose number

exceeds that of the sands of the sea, and whose charity gave forth a yet sweeter odour in death than in life.

(Ch. 87). This degree is the prize for the whole course of love, as the apostle says: 'Do you not know that all who run in a race, all indeed run, but only one receives the prize?'[532] He may well say 'only one', for I believe that there are few who have risen to this degree, since, according to Bernard, 'perfection is seldom found on earth'. He also says in his eighty-fourth sermon: 'I reckon this second to none amongst spiritual graces, since it ranks first amongst the gifts, but is the last to be acquired. It is consequent upon no virtue, and inferior to none. How could it indeed be inferior to any, seeing that it is rather the consummation of all?'[533]

I do not think, however, that this can happen unless the bridegroom linger over the kiss which he imprints upon the inebriated soul, that he may thus release her from prison to give praise unto his name.[534] On the other hand, when he bestows his kisses but intermittently, she is able to revive and return to this life, and so the spirit does not altogether leave the body. Let him who can take it, take it.[535] But things of this sort are to be learnt only from the book of experience, as Bernard declares in the third sermon, where he comments on the text: 'Let him kiss me with the kiss of his mouth' in the following words: 'I do not think that anyone can know what this kiss is unless he has received it.' This is not to be wondered at, seeing that it is 'the hidden manna', and they that eat it shall yet hunger,[536] and 'the fountain sealed up, of which no stranger may partake, but those that drink from it still thirst'.[537]

(Ch. 88). Furthermore, I do not think that anyone who does not love God can have a thorough knowledge of the words which speak of this kiss, for how can anyone really know them if he does not understand them? The same authority testifies to the fact that no one who does not love can understand such words, when, commenting in his seventy-ninth sermon on the text: 'Have you seen him whom my soul loveth?', he says: 'In vain does anyone who does not love try to listen to, or read, the song of love, for a heart that is cold cannot take in words that are on fire', and he gives the following illustration: 'Just as someone who does not know Greek cannot understand anyone speaking Greek, nor one who knows no Latin anyone speaking Latin, and so on; in the same way the language of love is unintelligible to one who does not love, and will be like "sounding brass or a tinkling cymbal".'[538]

If anyone then wishes to understand the words of love he must love, and if anyone wants to know about this kind of kiss, he must learn from experience.

This kiss is exceedingly sweet and unutterably delightful, nor are any of this world's pleasures to be compared with it, as I have heard from someone who had experienced such a thing in his own soul. It withdraws the senses from activity, and absorbs the intellect, so that for as long as it lasts, a man is altogether out of himself.

(Ch. 89).   Listen now to what Hugh, one of God's chosen servants, has to say about it in his *Betrothal Gift of the Soul*. At the end of that little book he speaks in the name of the soul, and asks himself:

> What is that lovely sensation which sometimes comes over me when I think of my spouse, and affects me so strongly and sweetly, that I am taken right out of myself and drawn away I know not whither? For all at once I feel renewed and completely changed, and I cannot describe the sense of well-being which then fills me. With conscience gladdened, and all the misery of past sorrow forgotten, I rejoice in spirit; my mind becomes clear, my heart is enlightened, and my desires find pleasure in fulfilment. In the state in which I find myself, I can think of no other. I seem to hold something within me in loving embrace, and though I know not what it is, I strive with all my might to hold it fast for ever, and never to let it go. My spirit is thus engaged as it were in a delightful struggle not to let what it holds depart, for it longs to embrace it for ever, finding therein an end to all its desires. It experiences supreme and unutterable joy, seeks naught else, covets naught else, but desires to remain like that for ever. Can it be that it is my beloved?

He answers as follows:

(Ch. 90). It is indeed your beloved, who has come to visit you, not in order to give himself to you completely, but to offer you a taste of himself. He holds out to you some of the first-fruits of his love, without fully revealing the plenitude of abundance. The most outstanding feature of your betrothal gift is the fact that he who will one day reveal himself to you plainly and give himself to you as your possession for ever sometimes offers you a taste of himself even now, in order that you may know how sweet he is.[539]

One who had tasted this sweetness afterwards besought the Lord with these words: 'Restore unto me the joy of thy salvation, and strengthen me with a perfect spirit.'[540] That is to say: 'Grant, as thou didst before, that I may once more know the delights of thy salvation, and, lest I should ever again commit such vile crimes, strengthen my heart with a perfect spirit.'

Another who had also experienced it says:

> I yearn, wherever I may be
> To have my Jesu's company;
> To find him is delight to me,
> To hold him, bliss in high degree.
>
> His kisses and embrace exceed
> The sweetness of the honeyed mead;
> To clasp Christ so is joy indeed,
> And yet such moments pass with speed.[541]

Let this suffice for the kiss of the spouse. I will go on now to speak a little about the excellence of the aforesaid novel kind of martyrdom, and then I will conclude.

(Ch. 91). Whoever reaches the summit of the ninth degree, which is death itself, has now fulfilled the law, once he is dead. He has run the way of God's commandments, and seen the end of all consummation.[542] Rightly is he placed with the highest order of angels, and those supreme princes, the Seraphim, claim him as a member of their company, because he is especially fitted for their function, which surpasses that of the other angels, and was conferred upon them as their prerogative. Hence St Gregory says in his thirty-fourth homily:

There are some who are so fired with the love of divine contemplation that they yearn for their Creator alone; no longer desiring anything of this world, they are nourished only by eternal love; relinquishing what is earthly and transcending in spirit all that is temporal, they are enkindled with fervent love, and in this very fervour they find rest; aflame with love themselves, they enkindle others by their speech, so that all who hear their words are straightway fired with love of God. Where else should such as these have been allotted a place by their vocation, if not among the number of the Seraphim?[543]

Thus far Gregory.

(Ch. 92). My heart is not able to conceive, nor my tongue to express,[544] the excellence of this form of martyrdom, but, in case I should seem to pass it over altogether, I will try to say something about it, not putting forward my own views presumptuously, but submitting them for correction to men who have studied such things, and have had experience of them.

According to the words of the prophet: 'The death of the saints is precious in the sight of the Lord';[545] no one, therefore, who lives a good life has a bad death, and even if such a one be suddenly overtaken by death, he will nevertheless be at rest.[546] Still more precious was the death undergone by the saints, when it entailed mockery and stripes, fetters and imprisonment. They were stoned, cut asunder, put to the proof of the sword, and died for Christ Jesus, our Lord.[547] How pleasing to God must we then believe that death to be which is brought about neither by fire, water, sword nor any element, but simply by the fire of divine love? And if we say that love is strong when it overcomes torments and will not yield to death itself, though death result from those torments, what shall I say of that love which, without any external violence intervening, itself causes the death of the individual of whom it has taken possession?

(Ch. 93). I should say for certain that such love is the acme of all perfection, the goal of all who run the course, and the consummation of the commandments. There can be nothing better, nothing more estimable, nothing more worth while, nothing more glorious, nothing more precious in the sight of the Lord.

I am not proved wrong by Christ and Augustine, when Christ says: 'Greater love than this no man hath, that a man lay down his life for his friends',[548] and Augustine: 'None have given so lavishly as those who have given themselves.'[549] My defence is this: what Christ says here applies to himself, and no love is comparable to his, since he alone, by laying down his life for his friends, delivered them from Satan's tyranny. As for what Augustine says, the reply to that is that 'None have given', and so on, must be understood of those who have departed this life at times when the Church enjoyed peace, such as the confessors and other faithful Christians, who did not shed their blood for Christ's sake, nor were urged to deny our Lord and worship the gods of the pagans, and who thus did not endure martyrdom for the word of truth. Augustine is not referring to those who succumb to the violence of love alone; they are to be held all the more truly martyrs, since they bear within them the very thing which brings about their death for Christ, and they stand in no need of a stroke from any sword to render them martyrs.

I would suggest that it was this most precious death which befitted our Lord's Mother and St John the Evangelist, and that they were perhaps preserved from death by the sword precisely in order that they might die later as martyrs of love. Whether this is so or not, I cannot tell, God knows, and I will not state as a fact something which merely seems probable both from reason and the evidence of authority.

(Ch. 94). Reason surely tells us that those who had been outstanding in merit should also have surpassed all others in their manner of dying. The Church affirms nothing more precise than that they did depart this life. I feel then all the more confident in maintaining my opinion, since I can find nothing to disprove it, and this gives me some support for my view, whether I be told they died or did not die. If they did die, as Jerome and Bede state in the martyrology used by the Church, then their death must have been due to some cause sufficient to separate the soul from the body, according to the definition of death. This cause must have been either joy or sorrow, since the Church declares that they died a death involving no physical suffering or pain, for they are said to have been as immune from the pangs of death as they were from concupiscence of the flesh. Their death must somehow have resulted from excess of joy or love. These two things are actually so inseparable that there can be no joy without love, nor love without joy. Medical men say that both dilate or widen the heart, and that the more intense they are the more they dilate it; if they are extremely intense they dilate it excessively, and so cause death.

Who would deny that Mary, the Mother of my Lord, had the greatest possible love for her Son, who was the supreme joy of her heart? The Church uses the Canticle of Canticles allegorically of our Lady, and its words breathe forth the fragrance of unutterable love to such an extent that, according to Bernard, they are unintelligible save to those themselves aflame with love.

(Ch. 95). Granted that she had attained to the highest degree of love possible in this life, given the absence of her Son, it may be reasonably assumed that when he returned to take her from this world, either she died of love and sheer joy, or else she was not till then in possession of the fullness of love possible in this life, for the presence of the beloved increases love as well as joy.

I think that the same is true of the apostle John, though I would not for a moment compare him with our Lord's Mother, who is unspeakably and incomparably superior to all others, whether men or women. Yet I do believe that none has imitated the purity of the Virgin so perfectly as he who took Christ's place as her guardian. He had much in common with our Lord's Mother, for they were closely related by blood, both were loved by Christ in a special way, and both were outstanding for their chastity. Our Lord's own word had made Mary John's mother, and him her son. After the death of Christ they lived together, surviving longer than any of the others, and neither was slain by the sword. Christ himself came to be present at the death of each, not a trace of the remains of either could be discovered where they were buried, but manna was found in their tombs, and thereupon both were believed to have been taken up by Christ our Lord into Heaven.

Since there was such similarity between them in all these points, it does not seem likely that their deaths were dissimilar, although we do not know for certain. There seems no reason to suppose that we are mistaken in assuming the most perfect thing of the most perfect people, when no authentic evidence can be found to the contrary. If our Lord would not have even the soul of a beggar dying on a dung-hill called forth, unaccompanied by David, playing upon his harp, what shall we not believe with regard to our Lord's Mother and John, both of whom were so especially dear to Christ?

(Ch. 96). Since, however, all know that these two are both in a special category, what can I say of one who is neither our Lord's Mother nor Christ's apostle, but who nevertheless passed out of this world in the way I described above?

If John Chrysostom is right in saying: 'Whoever despises the whole world is greater than all the world',[550] how can we estimate the value of one who not only despised the whole world, but himself as well, and endured a wonderful martyrdom for our Lord's sake? It seems to me true to say that such a man is worth more to the world than the world is worth to him, for all the world put together would not suffice him, and yet he can help the whole world. For the world was made for man, not man for the world, and as Hugh says in the *Betrothal Gift of the Soul*: 'The wicked exist, not for their own sake, but in order that they may try God's elect.'[551] If there were not a single just man left, the world would come to an end, and so, according to Augustine, as long as the world lasts there will not fail to be members of the dove,[552] even though they may be concealed in the clefts of the rock, and so hidden from our eyes.

(Ch. 97). O if only I knew one of God's friends, who was ever filled with ardent love for him, how gladly would I submit to his teaching, and how eagerly hearken to his glowing words! A heart on fire cannot but utter burning words, and a heart wounded by love muŝt needs wound others with its words. I know, Lord, and I know it well and truly, that from all eternity thou didŝt foresee such as would be wounded by the darts of thy love, and so thou didŝt take flesh. To redeem them thou didŝt choose to die, not that they had merited thine incarnation and death, as though anyone had first given to thee, and afterwards thou hadŝt made reŝtitution,[553] but it was rather by virtue of thy death that they were able to do what thou didŝt from all eternity foresee they would do. Thus thy death was due to no man on account of his preceding merits, but was itself the cause and origin of every meritorious act whatsoever.

And now in conclusion I beg thee, sweet Jesus, who art both the beginning and the end, grant that I myself may have such an end, that I may be numbered among the flock of thine eleĉt, and may so pass through the good things of this world that I may not at the laŝt lose those of the next.[554]

(Ch. 98). Remember, sweet Jesus, whom I seek to please, that it is thee I desire to love above all. Make me joyfully fulfil thy commands, so that I may see thy face for ever, and deal with me so mercifully before I die that I may know that I love nothing so much as God. May I be proteĉted by thy hand from all present evils, and find firm support in the sign of viĉtory. Ward off famine, foe and plague, grant us all-pervading peace, and, for the sake of tranquillity, cause the brethren to be of one mind. Put an end to wars, keep far from us the deadly injury of sin, leŝt souls rush headlong to perdition, be thou to us a tower of ŝtrength.

Pray proteĉt us, e'er direĉt us, and at death's decisive hour,
Stay prevailing, leŝt we failing should succumb to Satan's power.
    Fiends' disguises, wiles, surprises, banish from us far away,
    Leŝt they tear us and ensnare us, making us their helpless prey.
Saving power, Mary's flower, bear us up to Heaven high,
Where the seeing of God's Being will our longing satisfy.
                                                        Amen.

Here ends the Meditation addressed to Chriŝt crucified.

[Scripture references are to the Vulgate (and Douay version); liturgical references to the Roman Missal and Monastic Breviary.]

1. Gen. xviii, 27.   2. Cf. Is. vi, 5.   3. Ps. xlix, 16–17.
4. Cf. Hymn *Ut queant laxis* (feast of St John Baptist).
5. Cf. Ps. xvii, 36.
6. Cf. Offertory *Recordare* (22nd Sunday after Pentecost); Esth. xiv, 13.
7. Ps. i, 6.   8. Deut. ix, 18.   9. Tob. iii, 13.
10. Is. xxxviii, 17.   11. Cf. Ps. xxi, 23.   12. Cf. Ps. lxxi, 12.
13. Cf. Ps. lxxi, 12.   13a. Ps. xxix, 12.   14. Is. lii, 4.
15. Cf. Ezech. xxvii, 23.   16. Ps. cvi, 23.
17. Cf. Lk. i, 52; Is. xiv, 13.   18. Ps. cxii, 7; I Kings ii, 8.
19. Apoc. xii, 10.   20. Ps. lxxiii, 21.   21. Cf. Ps. lxxi, 14.
22. Cf. Antiphon *Senex puerum portabat* (feast of Purification B.V.M.).
23. Ps. xxxix, 7–8.
24. St Isidore, *Etymol.* lib. vii, c. vi; *PL* 82, 276.
25. Esth. xiii, 10.   26. Cf. Gen. ii, 2.   27. Lk. i, 72.
28. Cf. Gen. vi, 9.
29. Cf. St Augustine, *De Civitate Dei*, lib. xvi, c. ii; *PL* 41, 478–9.
30. Rom. x, 18.
31. Lk. vi, 31; *Rule of St Benedict*, c. iv.
32. St Isidore, *Etymol.* lib. vii, c. vi; *PL* 82, 276.
33. *Lexicon Origeniacum*, *PL* 23, 1282, and St Isidore, *loc. cit.*
34. Ps. cxviii, 96.   35. Rom. v, 5.   36. Rom. viii, 15.
37. Ps. cxviii, 32.   38. Gen. xxi, 6.   39. Gen. xxii, 13.
40. Cf. *Missale Romanum*, Preface of the Passion.
41. Jn. x, 14, 28.   42. I Pet. ii, 25.   43. Gen. xxvii, 29.
44. Lk. xxiii, 34.   45. I Cor. ii, 8.   46. Cf. Gen. xxxv, 10.
47. St Isidore, *Etymol.* lib. vii, c. vii; *PL* 82, 282; *Lexicon Graec. Nom. Hebraic. PL* 23, 1322.
48. Jn. i, 14.   49. Gen. ii, 23.
50. Cf. St Leo, *Epist.* 31, c. 2; *Sermo* 22, 2; *PL* 54, 791–2, 195.
51. Cf. *Symbolum Nicaeno-Constant. DB* 86.
52. Cf. Gen. xxxvii, 32.
53. Gen. xxxvii, 33; cf. St Bonaventure, *Lignum Vitae* (ed. Vives, t. xii, 78).
54. Cf. Jn. xix, 24; Cant. v, 7.   55. Job x, 22.
56. Cf. Gen. ii, 15.   57. Apoc. xiv, 13.   58. Ps. xxiii, 1.
59. Apoc. xix, 16.   60. Dan. iii, 100.   61. Mt. xxviii, 18.
62. Cf. Gen. xl, 14.   63. Gen. xxxvii, 27.
64. Cf. Gen. xlii, 25.   65. Jn. xii, 24–5.   66. Ps. cxliv, 16.
67. I Cor. i, 30.   68. Cf. I Jn. ii, 1–2. 69. Cf. Jer. xviii, 20.
70. Lk. xxii, 15.   71. Gen. xiv, 21.   72. Ps. lxxii, 25.
73. Ps. lxxvi, 6; Is. xxxviii, 15.   74. Num. xxi, 8–9.
75. Ps. ci, 8.   76. Ps. cii, 12.   77. Jn. i, 29.
78. Ex. xii, 6–8.
79. Antiphon *O quam suavis est* (feast of Corpus Christi).
80. Cf. Rom. viii, 32.   81. From the *Exultet* of Holy Saturday.
82. Heb. i, 3.   83. Cf. Wis. ii, 20.
84. Cf. Antiphon *Oblatus est* (Maundy Thursday).
85. Lk. xix, 21.   86. Is. liii, 9.   87. Cf. II Cor. v, 21.
88. Cf. Rom. v, 10.   89. Phil. ii, 8.   90. Cf. Rom. viii, 16.
91. Rom. viii, 9.   92. I Cor. xvi, 22.   93. I Jn. iv, 10; ii, 16.

94. Cf. Num. xi, 30–33, Ex. xvi, 11–13.
95. Apoc. ii, 17.   96. Ex. xvi, 18.   97. Ps. xxx, 20.
98. Judges xv, 15.   99. Mk. xi, 15.
100. St Isidore, *Etymol.* lib. vii, c. vi; *PL* 82, 278.
101. Ps. cvi, 16.   102. Cf. Judges xv, 4–5.
103. Ex. xv, 11.   104. Cant. ii, 15.   105. Gen. iii, 15.
106. Antiphon *Sicut novellae olivarum* (feast of Corpus Christi).
107. Cf. Mt. xxiv, 24.   108. I Cor. x, 13.   109. Eph. vi, 16.
110. Cf. *Glossa Ordinaria* on I Kings xvii, 16.
111. Rom. viii, 28.
112. Cf. *Fragmenta libri Nomin. Hebraic. PL* 23, 1246.
113. Hymn *Veni Creator.*   114. Is. ix, 6.   115. Jas. i, 17.
116. Jn. iii, 16.   117. Ps. xliv, 3.   118. II Kings i, 26.
119. Ps. lxxxviii, 35.   120. Is. xlix, 15.   121. Cf. I Kings xviii, 4.
122. Cf. St Isidore, *Etymol.* lib. vii, c. vi, *PL* 82, 279; St Jerome, *Liber Nominum Hebraicorum, PL* 23, 857.
123. Cant. i, 4.   124. Cf. Ps. xiii, 1.
125. Cf. Ps. cv, 23; Gen. vi, 6.
126. Cf. Ex. xxxii, 11, and Responsory *Recordare* (Matins of 4th Sunday after Pentecost).
127. Cf. Gen. i, 27.   128. Gen. iii, 5.   129. Wis. viii, 1.
130. Is. vi, 8.   131. Cf. II Cor. ix, 7.
132. Ps. xviii, 6.   133. Prov. viii, 31. 134. Tit. ii, 14.
135. Prov. xxi, 30.   136. Cf. Lk. xxiv, 39.
137. Rom. v, 10.   138. Cf. II Kings xxiii, 8.
138a. Mt. xvi, 16.   139. Is. lii, 3–5.
140. Ex. xxxii, 36; II Cor. xii, 1.
141. I Pet. i, 12.   141a. Cf. Jn. vii, 38.
142. Cf. Ps. cxlvi, 10.   143. Cf. Mt. xxvi, 38.
144. Cf. *Alleluia, Dulce lignum* (feast of Exaltation of the Holy Cross).
145. Cf. Lam. v, 1.   146. Jn. xix, 15. 146a. Mt. xxvii, 42.
147. Jn. vii, 12.   148. Mt. xxvii, 29. 149. Mt. xxvii, 40.
150. Ps. lxviii, 22.   151. Cf. Ps. cxv, 12–13.
152. I Cor. xii, 3.
153. Innocent III, *De Contemptu Mundi*, iii, 15; *PL* 217, 745.
154. Phil. ii, 5–10.   155. Ps. cx, 9.   156. Is. xlv, 24.
157. Cf. St Bernard, *De Diligendo Deo*, c. x and xv; *PL* 182, 992, 999–1000.
158. Cf. I Kings, iii, 9; Jas. i, 21.
159. Cf. Jn. iv, 16.   160. Lk. viii, 8; Apoc. ii, 7.
161. Ps. cxxvi, 3.   162. Cf. Lk. xviii, 34.
163. Cf. Ps. xv, 1.   164. Jn. xiv, 21.   165. Rom. vii, 18.
166. Hymn *Veni Creator.*
167. Cf. Collect *Deus cui omne cor patet* (Mass for asking grace of Holy Spirit).
168. Ps. l, 12.   169. Ps. lxx, 18.   170. Gen. vi, 3.
171. Job xv, 15.   172. Lam. iv, 5.   173. Mt. viii, 8.
174. Ps. xxxiii, 9.   175. Cf. Lk. xxiv, 30, 35.
176. Cf. Apoc. xix, 12.
177. Cf. Collect *Deus qui inter cetera* (Common of Virgin Martyrs).
178. Cf. Collect *Deus qui diligentibus te* (5th Sunday after Pentecost).
179. Mt. xxvi, 28.   180. Mt. xvi, 16; see above, ch. 13.
181. Cf. Wis. xi, 25.   182. Jas. i, 17.   183. Rom. ix, 21.
184. Cf. Ps. lxxii, 17.   185. Rom. xi, 33.   186. Cf. Ps. lxv, 5.

187. Ps. cxliii, 8.   188. Ps. lxxii, 1; Jer. ii, 13.
189. Deut. xxxii, 15; Ps. lxxxviii, 16.
190. Ps. xxxii, 12.   191. Ps. xci, 5.   192. Prov. xv, 15.
193. I Jn. iv, 18.   194. I Cor. ii, 2.   195. Wis. vii, 10.
196. Ps. cxliv, 9.
197. Cf. St Bernard, *Sermo xlii De Diversis*, 2; PL 183, 661.
198. Cf. Phil. ii, 7.   199. Gen. i, 1.   200. Baruch iii, 38.
201. Deut. xxxii, 18.
202. St Bernard, *Sermo XX in Cantica*; PL 183, 867; I Cor. xvi, 22.
203. Cf. Ps. xciii, 9.
204. Is. xlii, 14.   205. Cf. III Kings xviii, 27.
206. Ps. xiii, 1.   206a. Cf. Ps. cxli, 5.   207. Jn. viii, 50.
208. Cf. Job xiv, 13–14.   209. *Ibid.*   210. Cf. Is. xxxiii, 14.
211. Cf. St Bernard, *Sermo XI in Cantica*, 7; *Sermo XXVII De Diversis*, 6–8; PL 183, 827, 615–6.
212. Cf. Is. ix, 5.   213. Cf. Job x, 7.   214. Ps. cxxxviii, 8–10.
215. Phil. ii, 6.   216. Col. ii, 9.   217. Habacuc iii, 18.
218. Cf. Jer. xvii, 5.   219. Eph. iii, 12.   220. Cf. Acts x, 42.
221. Ps. xiii, 1.   222. I Jn. v, 16.   223. Heb. vi, 4.
224. Cf. Mt. vii, 20; Gal. v, 20–21; II Cor. ix, 7.
225. Unidentified.   226. I Cor. i, 13.   227. II Cor. xi, 23.
228. Prose *Salve Virgo singularis* (Dreves, *Analecta Hymnica*, xxxix, 48, no. 41b).
229. Cf. Collect *Deus qui salutis aeternae* (feast of Circumcision).
230. Lk. ii, 35.   231. Cf. Rom. iii, 23.
232. St Augustine, *De Gratia Christi*, xii, 13; PL 44, 367.
233. In reality St Peter Chrysologus, *Sermo* 50, PL 57, 503.
234. Cf. Gen. i, 13; Dan. xiii, 56.
235. Ps. xliii, 16.   236. Cf. Mt. vii, 3–5.
237. Cf. *Rule of St Benedict*, c. iv (*ad finem*).
238. Cf. II Cor. vi, 2.   239. I Jn. v, 16.
240. Cf. Responsory *Peccantem me* (Office of the Dead).
241. Unidentified; but cf. St Augustine, *De Civitate Dei*, lib. xxi, c. 24; PL 41, 737–8.
242. Heb. vi, 4–6; cf. Rom. vi, 8–10.
243. Cf. St Thomas, *Summa Theologica*, iii, 84, 10.
244. Tit. iii, 4–5.   245. Cf. Apoc. vi, 16.   246. Lk. iii, 7.
247. Ps. lix, 6.   248. Jn. x, 9.   249. Mt. xi, 28.
250. Cf. St Augustine, *Enarratio in Ps. lxxiv*, PL 36, 953.
251. Ps. xxxiii, 6.   252. Lk. xvii, 14.   253. Dan. iii, 40.
254. Ps. lix, 6.   255. Cf. Mal. iv, 2; Ps. lvi, 2.
256. Cf. Gen. ix, 12–17.   257. Cf. Gal. iv, 2–4.
258. Lk. xxi, 25.   259. Cf. Ps. cxxvii, 1.   260. Cf. Is. xi, 12.
261. Cf. Jn. viii, 47.   262. Lk. viii, 10.   263. Mt. xii, 39.
264. Cf. I Kings, xxi, 5.   265. I Cor. iii, 7.
266. Cf. Job xlii, 3; Ps. xxi, 3.   267. Jn. iii, 8.
268. Cf. St Ambrose, *Homiliae in Lucam*, lib. ii, c. i; PL 15, 1640.
269. Ps. lxvii, 22.   270. Gen. ii, 24.   271. Is. lxvi, 8.
272. Cf. Antiphon *Medicinam carnalem* (feast of St Agatha).
273. Ps. xviii, 11.   274. Cf. Is. lxvi, 11.   275. Jn. vi, 54.
275a. Deut. viii, 3.   276. Cf. Jn. vi, 64.
277. Cf. Antiphon *Oblatus est* (Maundy Thursday).
278. Cf. Ps. cxxxiv, 6.   279. Mk. xiv, 45.   280. Mk. x, 16.

281. Ezech. i, 3.   282. Heb. i, 1.
283. Cf. II Cor. iii, 6; Heb. vii, 19.
284. Ex. iii, 6; the manuscript has *Israel* for *Isaac.*
285. Ps. lxxv, 1.   286. Ps. xvii, 10.   287. Jn. vi, 57.
288. Cf. Antiphon *O Rex gentium* (December 22) and Eph. ii, 14.
288a. Ezech. i, 10.
289. St Gregory, *Homilia in Ezechielem,* lib. i, hom. iv; *PL* 76, 816.
290. Ps. xv, 11 and xciii, 18.
291. Ps. xv, 4.   292. Rom. v, 5.   293. Cant. i, 1.
294. Ps. xviii, 5.   295. Rom. v, 5.   296. Gal. iv, 6.
297. Rom. viii, 9.   298. I Jn. iv, 8.   299. Jn. xv, 6.
300. Deut. xxxi, 13.   301. Cf. Apoc. ii, 17.   302. Mt. xiii, 45–46.
303. St Gregory, *Homilia XI in Evangelia; PL* 76, 1115.
304. Cf. II Cor. xi, 21.   305. Is. liii, 1.   306. Is. lii, 10.
307. Ps. xcvii, 2.   307a. Mk. xvi, 5.
308. St Gregory, *Homilia XXI in Evangelia, PL* 76, 1170.
309. Cant. ii, 6.   310. Prov. iii, 16.
311. St Augustine, *Epistola* 194 *ad Sixtum; PL* 33, 880.
312. Is. xxvi, 12.   313. I Cor. iv, 7.   314. Prov. iii, 16.
315. Ps. cxi, 3.   316. Cf. Ps. xcii, 5.
317. Antiphon xi of Matins of Trinity Sunday.
318. Cf. I Cor. iii, 11; II Cor. iii, 18.
319. Cf. Ps. lxxxviii, 7.   320. I Jn. iii, 2.
321. Responsory *Ipsi sum desponsata* (feast of St Agnes).
322. I Pet. i, 12.   323. Jn. xvii, 3; xiv, 21.
324. Jn. xiv, 21.   325. Is. lxiv, 4.   326. I Cor. ii, 9.
327. St Augustine, *De Libero Arbitrio,* lib. iii, c. xxv; *PL* 32, 1308.
328. Ps. xxxv, 9.   329. Prov. xi, 25.   330. Ps. xli, 3.
331. Ps. lxxxvi, 7.   332. Eph. v, 29–32; Gen. ii, 23.
333. Jn. xv, 4.   334. Cf. Jn. vi, 37.
335. Cf. Ps. xxxi, 7; ix. 10.   336. Cf. I Pet. ii, 22.
337. Cf. Is. liii, 9; Ps. xxi, 10–11.
338. Jn. iii, 3.   339. Phil. iv, 3.   340. Cf. Lam. iv, 5.
341. Cf. Ps. cxliii, 8; Is. vi, 5.
342. Cf. Is. xii, 3; Jn. iv, 11.
343. Col. i, 19.   344. Gen. ix, 22.   345. Lk. v, 8.
346. Responsory *Peccata mea* (Sundays after Epiphany).
347. Mt. ix, 12.   348. Jn. vii, 39.   349. Cf. Mt. xvi, 21–3.
350. Cf. Ecclus. xiii, 1.   351. Rom. viii, 35.   351a. Cf. Is. lxv, 2.
352. Prov. i, 24–x.   353. Ps. cxxix, 4; l, 9.   354. Gen. xiii, 9.
355. Cf. Mt. xvii, 4.   356. Cf. Prov. viii, 31.
357. Jn. vi, 37.   358. Cf. Jn. xii, 26; xiv, 21.
359. Ps. xxx, 21.   360. Cant. ii, 14.   361. Apoc. xvii, 15.
362. Cf. Ps. xciv, 7.   363. I Pet. ii, 9.   364. Ps. cv, 10.
365. Eccles. i, 7.   366. Cf. Jn. x, 28.   367. Cf. Lk. xi, 21.
368. Cf. Mt. xxii, 16.   369. I Pet. v, 7.
370. Cf. Richard Rolle, *English Writings* (ed. H. E. Allen), 36.
371. Cited in *Chapters of English Black Monks* (ed. W. A. Pantin), ii, 131;
     cf. St Augustine, *Sermo* 75, ii, 2 (*PL* 38, 475), and *Sermo* 362, vii,
     7 (*PL* 39, 1615).
372. Apoc. x, 9.   373. Ecclus. i, 18.   374. Is. xxviii, 19.
375. Col. i, 24.   376. I Cor. ii, 2.
377. Cf. Jos. i, 8; Wis. ix, 10.

378. Cf. Ps. xviii, 4; xxix, 12.
379. Cf. Ps. xlix, x; l, x: Jn. v, 22.   380. Cf. Rom. xv, 4.
381. Cf. St Bernard, *De Diligendo Deo*, c. 1 and 6; *PL* 182, 974, 983.
382. Ps. lxxiii, 23.   383. Ps. cxxxviii, 21.   384. Jn. xv, 14.
385. Ps. cxxxviii, 20.   386. Jn. xv, 24.   387. Jn. ix. 22.
388. St Augustine, *De Sermone Domini in Monte*, xiv, 47; *PL* 34, 1290;
     cf. Mt. vi, 24.
389. St Augustine, *Liber Primus Retractationum*, c. 19, no. 8; *PL* 32, 617;
     cf. Ps. lxxiii, 23.
390. Deut. vi, 5; Mt. xxii, 38.   391. Cf. I Jn. ii, 4.
392. Jn. xiv, 24; Lk. xi, 23.
393. Antiphon *Posuit signum* (feast of St Agnes).
394. Ex. iv, 4.
395. St Bernard, *Sermo XX in Cantica*; *PL* 183, 867.
396. I Cor. xvi, 22.   397. Cant. v, 10.
398. Cf. Ps. xliv, 3; lxxii, 28; Jer. xvii, 5.
399. St Bernard, *Sermo XX in Cantica*; *PL* 183, 870.
400. Cant. ii, 14; Ps. l, 10.   401. Jn. x, 27.
402. Jn. vi, 69.   403. Jn. viii, 47.   404. Ps. lxxx, 12.
405. Ps. xvii, 45.
406. St Bernard, *Sermo XX in Cantica*; *PL* 183, 870.
407. Lam. i, 13.   408. Ps. lxxxiii, 3.   409. Gal. ii, 20.
410. Cf. Col. iii, 5.   411. Cf. Gal. v, 24.
412. St Bernard, *Sermo XX in Cantica*; *PL* 183, 869, 871.
413. Cf. I Cor. xii, 31.   414. Ps. cxviii, 91.
415. Not in Holy Scripture, but cited as such by St Gregory, *Homilia
     XXXVIII in Evangelia*, no. 2; *PL* 76, 1282.
416. Cf. Ps. i, 2.   417. Wis. ix, 10.   418. II Tim. ii, 4.
419. Ps. cxviii, 99–100.
420. Cf. St Bernard, *Sermo III in festo Pentecostes*; *PL* 183, 332.
421. Cf. *Vita Prima S. Bernardi*; *PL* 185, 240.   422. Jn. vii, 34.
423. Job v, 14.   424. Cf. Gal. iv, 31.   425. Ps. xxxiii, 3.
426. St Gregory, *Homilia 27 in Evangelia*; *PL* 76, 1207; cf. St Bernard,
     Sermo XXIX de Diversis, *PL* 183, 620.
427. I Jn. ii, 27.   428. Cf. I Cor. i, 19.
429. Hymn *Veni Creator* and Jn. xiv, 26.
430. Jn. xiv, 26.   431. Jn. xvi, 7, 16–8.   432. Jn. xvi, 5.
433. Jn. xiv, 28.   433a. Jn. xvi, 27.
434. St Bernard, *Sermo XX in Cantica*; *PL* 183, 869.
435. Jn. xvi, 20.
436. Cf. *The Golden Legend*, Life of St Peter (29 June).
437. St Gregory, *Homilia XXX in Evangelia*; *PL* 76, 1221.
438. Cf. Lk. xii, 47–8.   439. II Cor. ix, 7.   440. Rom. xii, 8.
441. St Gregory, *Homilia XXVII in Evangelia*; *PL* 76, 1205.
442. Ecclus. xxxv, 11.
443. Hymn to St Cuthbert *Magnus Miles* (Dreves, *Analecta Hymnica*, xi
     103, no. 173).
444. Cf. I Pet. iii, 21.   445. Prov. xv, 13.   446. Prov. xv, 15.
447. Cf. Geoffrey of Durham, *Vita S. Bartholomaei de Farne*, § 10 in Symeon
     of Durham, *Opera* (RS), i, 302.
448. II Cor. i, 12.
449. St Bede, *Vita S. Cuthberti*, c. xvi; cf. B. Colgrave, *Two Lives of
     St Cuthbert*, 210.

450. Prov. xii, 21.   451. Ps. xxxvi, 24.   452. Rom. viii, 35–9.
453. Ps. cxviii, 57.   454. Cf. Ps. xviii, 11. 455. Cf. Gen. xxix, 20.
456. Cf. Ps. cxviii, 4, 127, 162.
457. Cf. Ps. lxi, 11.   457a. Jn. xiv, 23.
458. St Gregory, *Homilia XXX in Evangelia*; PL 76, 1221.
459. Lk. xvi, 13.
460. St Bede, *Expositio in Lucam*, lib. ii, c. xvi; PL 92, 531.
460a. Jn. x, 23.
461. St Gregory, *Homilia V in Evangelia*; PL 76, 1094.
462. Cf. *Rule of St Benedict*, c. i.
463. Mt. xix, 27.   464. Mt. vii, 15.   465. Cf. Mt. xv, 8.
466. Is. xxxviii, 17.   467. Cant. i, 5.
468. St Augustine, *Epistola* 78; PL 33, 272.
469. Unidentified. In the margin of the MS. a late hand has written *Non
     Gregorius*.
470. Phil. iv, 12.   471. Cf. Mt. vi, 21.
472. Ps. xxxiii, 10.   473. Ps. lxxii, 25.
474. Cf. Sixth lesson of St Edmund's feast in the Sarum Breviary (ed.
     Procter and Wordsworth, ii, 1057).
475. Phil. iii, 20.
476. In reality St Bernard, *De Praecepto et Dispensatione*, 60; PL 182, 892.
477. I Cor. iii, 1–2.   478. I Cor. ii, x.   479. I Cor. xiii, 1.
480. Peter the Lombard, *Liber Sententiarum*, lib. iii, dist. xxvii; PL 192, 812.
481. Mt. xxii, 40.   482. Is. lviii, 7.   483. Eph. v, 29.
484. St Gregory, *Homilia XVII in Evangelia*; PL 76, 1139.
485. I Jn. iv, 16.
486. St Gregory, *Homilia XXX in Evangelia*; PL 76, 1220.
487. Hugh of St Victor, *De Laude Charitatis*; PL 176, 975.
488. St Augustine, *De Trinitate*, lib. xii, c. xiv; PL 42, 1000–1.
489. Cf. I Cor. ii, 6.   490. Rom. viii, 28.
491. St Augustine, *In Epistolam Iohannis*, tr. vii, c. iv; PL 35, 2033.
492. II Cor. iii, 17.   493. Rom. viii, 8.   494. Lk. xi, 34.
495. St Bede, *Expositio in Lucam* in h. 1.: PL 92, 482.
496. I Cor. xiii, 4.   497. I Cor. x, 31.   498. I Thess. v, 17.
499. Cf. Responsory *Abscondite* (1st Sunday of Lent).
500. Cant. viii, x.   501. Cf. Ps. ii, 12.   502. Phil. i, 21.
503. Cant. ii, 5.   504. Cant. v, 8.   505. Cant. ii, 1.
506. Cant. i, 1.
507. St Bernard, *Sermo LI in Cantica*; PL 183, 1025.
508. Prov. xiii, 12.   509. Phil. i, 23.
510. Rom. vii, 24.   511. Cf. II Tim. i, 12.
512. Cf. Hymn *Doctor egregie* (feast of Conversion of St Paul).
513. Cf. I Cor. xiii, 12.   514. II Tim. iv, 6.
515. Cf. Ps. cii, 5.   516. Cant. ii, 12.   517. Ps. xxxvii, 10.
518. St Bernard, *Sermo LIX in Cantica*; PL 183, 1063.
519. Hymn *Dulcis Iesu memoria* (feast of Holy Name of Jesus; cf.
     Ephemerides Liturgicae, lvii, 1943 *passim*).
520. Cf. Ecclus. xxxi, 10.
521. Hymn *Beata nobis gaudia* (Lauds of Whitsunday).
522. St Augustine, *Liber de Perfectione Justitiae*, c. viii, ix; PL 44, 299, 302.
523. St Bernard, *De Diligendo Deo*, c. x, 29; PL 182, 992.
524. Cant. viii, 6.
525. John Pecham, *Philomena*, (Dreves, *Analecta Hymnica*, l, 602, n. 898).

526. Ps. lxxii, 26.
527. Ps. xxxii, 15 and *Glossa Ordinaria in h. l.*
528. Ps. lxxxiii 3, and *Glossa Ordinaria in h. l.*
529. Cf. *Acta S. Agnetis* (Mombritius, *Sanctuarium*, i, 41).
530. Unidentified.
531. St Bernard, *Sermo LXXIX in Cantica*; PL 183, 1163.
532. I Cor. ix, 24.
533. St Bernard, *Sermo LXXXIV in Cantica*, PL 183, 1184–5.
534. Cf. Ps. cxli, 8.　　　535. Mt. xix, 12.
536. Cf. Ecclus. xxiv, 29.
537. St Bernard, *Sermo III in Cantica*; PL 183, 794; cf. Eccles, xxiv, 29.
538. I Cor. xiii, 1; St Bernard, *Sermo LXXIX in Cantica*; PL 183, 1163.
539. Hugh of St Victor, *De Arrha Animae*; PL 176, 970.
540. Ps. l, 14.
541. Hymn *Dulcis Iesu memoria.*　　　　　542. Ps. cxviii, 32, 9x.
543. St Gregory, *Homilia XXXIV in Evangelia*; PL 76, 1253.
544. Hymn *Dulcis Iesu memoria.*　　　　　545. Ps. cxv, 15.
546. Cf. Wis. iv, 7.　　　547. Cf. Heb. xi, 36–7. 548. Jn. xv, 13.
549. St Augustine, *Sermo* 31, ii, 2; *PL* 38, 193.
550. Unidentified.
551. Hugh of St Victor, *De Arrha Animae*; PL 176, 958.
552. St Augustine, *Enarratio in Psalmum LIV*, 9; PL 36, 634–5; cf. Cant. ii, 14.
553. Cf. Rom. xi, 35.
554. Cf. Collect *Protector in te sperantium* (3rd Sunday after Pentecost).

Meditation by the same author addressed to the Blessed Virgin Mary, Mother of God

(Ch. 1). Before I begin to speak of our Lord's Mother, let me quietly consider within my soul who I am, of what stock I come, with how much intelligence and with what command of language I am gifted, and with what grace endowed. For how should the mouth of a sinner, sprung from the race of Canaan, of one dull-witted and slow of speech, possessed of neither grace nor merit, presume to utter a word about her who is the sublimity of heaven and the riches of the earth, despoiler of hell and pride of the heavenly court; who is at once the pledge of man's security and the terror of demons, queen of heaven, mistress of the world and empress of hell, who while being an object of the angels' veneration, is also the refuge of mortals and a safeguard against the devil; the daughter of the eternal Father, the Mother of God's Only-begotten Son and the temple of the Holy Ghost, amongst all creatures the one flower, whose fruit he was who made all creatures? All that I might wish to say has certainly been said already by the orthodox fathers, and merely to repeat the same things with my own lips would seem foolish, but if I speak in my own words, shall I not fall short of adequate praise?

Since whichever course I follow I am either ashamed or afraid, do thou intervene, O Virgin Mother, of whom I do indeed acknowledge myself unworthy to speak. Give me milk to drink from the breast that nourished my Lord, that I may drink my fill at Mary's bosom, for I am but a child, confronted with so difficult a task. Then indeed will my lips praise the Mother of my Lord and the words of my mouth magnify her, when the tongue of thy poor servant has tasted the stream, flowing from the abundance of thy grace.

(Ch. 2). Thou art she with whom no other virgin can be compared; thou who art so great that thy greatness cannot be expressed. Thou art indeed an opening into heaven, dawn of the eternal Sun, gate of the true paradise, and ark of the covenant. Thou holdest dominion over kings, and art the beauty of women, the pearl of virgins, light of ages and joy of the angels, consolation of the afflicted, refuge of sinners and restoration of all the faithful. But these, as thou knowest, my Lady, are Augustine's words, not mine.[1]

What shall I say of thee, Virgin Mother of our Lord, who alone hast attained virginal fruitfulness and fruitful virginity? It is a thing incomprehensibly great that thou shouldst be both virgin and mother, but incomprehensibly greater still it is that thou, daughter of the Father, shouldst be mother, not merely of any man, but of the Only-begotten, that is of the Son of God. It is to this that the Church is referring, when she sings:

> Thee and no other
> God chose as mother
> Of his Son, thus made thy brother,
>   Whose own daughter thou wast still.
> God's grace availed thee,
> Sin ne'er assailed thee,
> God sending to thee thus hailed thee:
>   Hail, who hast of grace thy fill![2]

Great love indeed did God show for thee, O Lady, in choosing thee to be the genuine mother of God. Thou didst thus become the royal palace of the Father, the bridal-chamber of the Son, and the abiding-place of the Holy Ghost. Thou dost enjoy an intimate relationship with God and with each of the Persons of the Blessed Trinity, being the mother of the self-same Son of whom God the Father is Father; with God the Son, whose Mother thou art; and also with God the Holy Ghost, through whose operation thou didst conceive thy Son. It was his strength that overshadowed thee;[2a] no element of sensual pleasure entered in. The fire of God's love completely consumed every trace of the results of original sin within thee.†
All at once thy heart was aglow, and in a twinkling of an eye thou didst bear within thy womb the Son of God. And so,

---

† At the time when the author wrote, the doctrine of our Lady's Immaculate Conception was not defined as of faith, but as a matter of theological opinion. See p. 24.

whatever good there is in the world comes from thee, from whom proceeds the dawn of our salvation.

(Ch. 3). In thee, dear Lady, God accomplished that new thing upon the earth, which long before, by the mouth of Jeremias, he had promised to bring about, namely that a woman should encompass a man.[3] Within thee human nature was united to God in one person, in such a way that he who was God was also man; he that was man, also God. In the tabernacle of thy womb there rested for nine months all the plenitude of the Godhead in bodily form,[4] and at the end of that time there came forth, though the door of thy womb remained closed, one who is beautiful beyond the sons of men[5] and far more lovable than the love of women[6]; proceeding from his bridal-chamber, he rejoiced as a giant to run the course[7] of our sad, penal condition, that he might make us sharers in his divinity.[8] Thou, Lady, art the ark of both Covenants, which contains the book of the law, the manna, and Aaron's rod.[8a] For thou dost contain the book of the law, since thy life is the very fullness of the law and the summit of all perfection. During the three days in which thy Son lay dead, the faith of the whole Catholic Church remained unshaken in thee, O blessed Lady, though it was tottering even in the hearts of the apostles. In thee, my Lady, was placed that manna, delicious as bread, and the food of the angels, our Lord Jesus Christ, upon whom the angels ever desire to gaze[9] for very love of his beauty. Thou art the rod which blossomed and put forth leaves, and bore the sweetest fruit, whence the Church sings of thee: 'The Virgin Mother of God is the rod.'[10]

(Ch. 4). Thou alone amongst women couldst once say to God: 'Thou art my Son, this day have I given birth to thee',[11] or again: 'He is bone of my bone and flesh of my flesh.'[12] From this it is clear to me that no one can ever adequately praise thee. Who could ever adequately praise thy soul, since thy flesh has been raised by God to such a degree of honour as to be joined to God in personal union, and the Word has been made flesh, assuming no other flesh than that of Jesus, which according

5+

to Augustine, in a sermon on the Assumption of the Blessed
Virgin, is the flesh of Mary? He says there: 'The flesh of Jesus
is the flesh of Mary, whom he has exalted above the stars.'[13]
But the flesh of Jesus is God, because the Word has been made
flesh; therefore Mary's flesh is God.†

Since, O Lady, it is the spirit which gives life,[14] and con-
sequently is more profitable, more noble, and worthy of greater
love and reverence, who could conceive praise worthy of thy
spirit, seeing that praise of thy flesh exceeds the capacity even
of the angelic intellect? For thy flesh has been assumed by God
in personal union, so that God has become man, and just as he
is God, begotten of the substance of the Father before all ages,
so also is he man, born of the substance of his Mother in
time.[15]

O wondrous woman, whose flesh may be adored without
blame,‡ for it is the foot-stool of the feet of the Lord, and holy
in all truth.[16] A carnal heart should not search further into these
things, and defiled lips must not presume to speak of the sublimity of thy soul, for it is a cause of wonder even to the
Cherubim and Seraphim that the Word should have been made
flesh, assuming no other flesh than that of Jesus, which is the
flesh of Mary. In Christ the integrity of both natures remained
unimpaired, that is of both the divine and the human, nor was
there any intermingling of these natures, for we must not
believe that Christ's divinity is his humanity, nor conversely
that his humanity is his divinity, although this ineffable union
of natures in one person is such that a man may be said to be
God, and God a man, God may be called flesh, and flesh God,
according to what is written: 'He is man, and who will recognize him?'[17] And again:

> Flesh having sinned, flesh doth atone,
> And God made flesh reigns on God's throne.[18]

---

†As will be seen in ch. 6, p. 123, the author's intention in writing this
astonishing sentence was orthodox. 'Mary's flesh' is here understood not
as her own body but as the humanity of our Lord Jesus Christ. He was
and always remained both Son of God and son of Mary.

‡To say that 'Mary's flesh' may be adored without blame would be
heretical if the author meant it of 'the flesh which Mary retains in her own
body', but he intends it here as synonymous with our Lord's humanity.
See preceding note, and pp. 23-4.

(Ch. 5).   I think that the question as to what special honour God accords to the soul of his Mother or what further reward he bestows upon it, is a very puzzling one and among God's greatest secrets, for since he has assumed her very flesh into personal union with himself, her own soul playing its part in the operation, what may we not believe about this soul which, as we have said, deserves still greater honour, and has a capacity for yet more abundant glory?

So it is, my Lady, that if anyone were to ask me who thou art, I should tell them that thou art the Virgin Mary, Mother of my Lord Jesus Christ. If I were asked what thou art like, I should answer that thou art humble as a handmaid, a faithful, worthy and most chaste virgin, fair as the moon, peerless as the sun, terrible as an army in array.[19] But if the question were how great thou art, I should reply that I do not know, since thou art so great that thy greatness surpasses description. Why so? Because thou didst bear in thy womb him whom the very heavens cannot contain,[20] as it is written: 'Virgin Mother of God, he whom the whole world does not suffice to contain became man, and enclosed himself within thy womb.'[21]

(Ch. 6).   I know not, O Lady, how to praise thee more highly, nor do I think that I shall ever be able to say more in thine honour than I have already said, for whatever else I can think of in praise of thee falls short of what has been said already: 'Thy flesh is God.' If I proclaim thee to be a virgin and the mother of our Lord, both these titles while being attributed to thine entire person, imply less than actual incorporation with the divinity; for although thou art both virgin and mother, thou art not joined to God in personal union, as is the flesh which God's Only-begotten Son took from thee and which was part of thyself.

I am then justified in saying: 'Thy flesh is God', because the Word was made flesh,[21a] not that flesh which thou dost retain in thine own body, but that which thou dost possess in thy Son, for it will never cease to be thine own flesh, since he will never cease to be thine own Son.

As for uttering worthy praise of thy soul, that I neither can do nor know how it could be done, for I believe its state to be ineffable, surpassing the understanding of every creature, save only the mind of Christ and thine own, for thou hast experimental knowledge of thine own beatitude.

Bow down thine ear, O Lady, to the prayers of thy suppliants, give ready hearing to their petitions, and extend to all the compassion for which they hope. May all who make this meditation experience thy consolation.[22]

(Ch. 7).   I beseech thee, my Lady, intercede with thy Son for me, that he may accept what I offer, grant what I ask and forgive what causes me fear. Through thee, O Lady, may he bestow on me bodily chastity, and make me little in my own eyes. May he dispel all blindness of heart, that I may know what is pleasing in his sight.

May remembrance of his name be my heart's great treasure,
    Lest the lust for worldly wealth should my soul endanger;
May he grant of grace on earth such abundant measure,
    That from heaven I may be no excluded stranger.
Let him guard me, lest I stray into grave temptation,
    Whence there might be no escape for my soul's securing;
May he ever strengthen me 'gainst such provocation,
    That at no time may I yield to the fiend's alluring.
May he strip my soul of love for the things that perish,
    Keep me lest I be deceived, to men's praise attending;
Let me but his sweetness taste, and with fervour cherish,
    Thus shall I all else despise, earthly joys transcending.
Do thou, Lady, win me faith that will stand unshaken,
    And will ne'er, deceived at last, err in any manner;
Buoy my heart with thoughts of bliss, hope therein awaken,
    That at judgement I may hold fast salvation's banner.
Grant me so to love my Lord, as to give him pleasure
    In whatever I may do, naught to him preferring.
May I e'er bewail my sins, contrite in such measure,
    That I never find again these same sins recurring.
Lead us, Queen of virgins, thou, up to God's high dwelling,
    Where we may be ever glad, true life apprehending;
Show us then thy wondrous face, fair beyond all telling,
    Shining with the radiant light of a dawn unending.
Do thou, noble Mother, now hear us orphans crying
    From the slough of misery. Turn in our direction;
For through thee our fragile life, prone through sin to dying,

Finds its strength against all ills by divine protection.
Thou, God's Mother, to us all hope indeed hast given,
  Since our Saviour, born of thee, wrought our reparation,
Ransoming what Eve had lost, into error driven,
  When through Satan's guile she fell, vanquished by temptation.
Humble Maiden, wise of heart, free from any tainting,
  Hear thy suppliants' voices now, as they fondly greet thee;
Ward from scourge this sorry race, stricken now and fainting,
  Deign thou all our ills to heal, humbly we entreat thee.

Virgin of all virgins kind, Mary be attentive
  To the prayers now offered up by those in affliction.
Show them how to turn from sin, be a glad incentive,
  Pattern thou of holiness, fraught with benediction.
Thou the rod of Jesse art, kind and loving Mother;
  With these verses I thy grace fain would be attaining.
Come and help us; tarry not; hope we have no other,
  Thou who didst alone conceive, virgin still remaining.
Gate of light, to thee we owe sunshine's true arriving,
  Vessel full of purity, Virgin Mother peerless;
Loose mankind from bonds of sin, that all evil striving
  May itself be crucified, rendering us fearless.
Once there was a certain man, poet skilled in diction,
  Living under Austin's rule, versed in holy learning;
He was known as Lubucus, author of no fiction,[23]
  And composed the lines below, thy high state discerning.

'Thou rod from Jesse springing, hear me thy praises singing, most
    loving Mother mine.
  Holy Mary, I declare thee virgin from all blemish free,
  By no other made a mother, save by God's divine decree.
For thou, God's word receiving, and thus his Son conceiving,
    hast won us peace divine.
  From thee gleaming, through thee streaming, came to us the
    light of grace,
  Thou the dawning of the morning, heralding the true sun's
    face.
For with thy flesh was shrouded, thus sweetly overclouded, that
    star, surpassing fine.
  Earth esteems thee, heaven deems thee worthy of the highest
    praise.
  Love we offer, praise we proffer; cleanse us, stained by evil
    ways.
In death aid our endeavour, that we may share for ever that
    blessed life of thine.   Amen.'

Notes to Meditation addressed to the Blessed Virgin

1. In reality these titles are found in the works of St Augustine, St Fulgentius, Ps-Augustine, etc.
2. Sequence *Benedicta es caelorum regina* (Dreves, *Analecta Hymnica* liv, 396, no. 252).

2a. Cf. Lk. i, 35. 3. Jer. xxxi, 22. 4. Cf. Col. ii, 9.
5. Ps. xliv, 3. 6. Cf. II Kings, i, 26. 7. Ps. xviii, 6.

8. Cf. Preface for feast of the Ascension.
8a. Cf. Deut. x, 1–5; Heb. ix, 4.
9. Cf. I Pet, i, 12.
10. Cf. Responsory *Stirps Jesse* (formerly on feast of Nativity B.V.M.).
11. Ps. ii, 7. 12. Gen. ii, 23.
13. Ps-Augustine, *De Assumptione B.M.V.* c. 5; PL 40, 1145.
14. Jn. vi, 64.
15. Cf. St Leo, *Sermo XXII*, 2; *Sermo XXVII*, 2; PL 54, 195, 217.
16. Cf. Ps. xcviii, 5.
17. Cf. Jer. xvii, 9; Eccles. viii, 16.
18. Hymn *Aeterne rex altissime* (Matins of feast of Ascension).
19. Cf. Cant. vi, 9.
20. Cf. Responsory *Sancta et immaculata* (feast of Circumcision).
21. Hymn *Virgo Dei genitrix* (Chevalier, *Repertorium Hymnologicum* no. 21764).
21a. Jn. i, 14.
22. Cf. Ps-Augustine, *Sermo CCVIII De Assumptione B.M.V.*; PL 39, 2134.
23. The reading of the MS. at this point *doctor ciuis lubucus* is corrupt, and the author referred to has not been identified.

Meditation addressed to the Angels by the same author

(Ch. 1). How great, O Lord, is the abundance of that sweetness which thou hast shown towards the men of thy right hand![1] Thou dost afford them the protection of angels from heaven,[2] who have so ardent a love for us that they keep us in all our ways, and bear us up in their hands, lest we dash our foot against a stone.[3] And though it is to thee, Lord, King of ages, immortal, invisible and only God that all honour and glory are due from us for all thy blessings,[4] yet it is right that we should also humbly and devoutly render thanks to those who day by day from dawn till eventide[5] watch over our interests. They are by nature superior to us since they are not composite, they are not sinners, and they preceded us in time, for before the mountains came into being, or the earth or universe were made, they were created[6]; the deep seas did not yet exist when they came into being, and when thou didst fashion the heavens, they were there, rendering all service to thee.[7] By that I do not mean that the invisible, angelic nature was actually created before the formless matter of visible things in the order of time. They both came into being at the same moment, since he who abides for ever created all things together. Angelic nature has, rather, a certain priority of honour, for before any of the things created during the six days had as yet a distinct existence or shape of their own, or had taken up their position in the universe, the angels were already exulting in the presence of God, and serving him in all things.[8]

Thou hast crowned them with honour and glory, O Lord, and when thou didst come down for the sake of us men and of our salvation thou didst make thyself a little less than them. Thou hast set them over the works of thy hands both by rank and tutelage.[9] When the apostate angels fell away, these did not side with them, but, afire with love for thee, they were consumed with longing to abide with thee and to have thee abiding within them.[10]

(Ch. 2).   After creating them, O Lord, thou didst establish
them in such a sublime state, that for the future they could
never be, or desire to be, aught else but eager for good.[10a] We
can learn how much we owe them from those with whom we
are contending, that is to say from the principalities and
powers, the rulers of this world of darkness,[11] who would
certainly kill us immediately on finding us in a state of mortal
sin, were it not that our warrior guardians resist them. As it is,
when we are tempted, these splendid champions of ours rise
up at God's command in our defence, and do not allow us to
be tempted beyond our strength, but make the issue of the
temptation such that we are able to hold our own and not be
led into temptation by the demons.[12]

Our harper sings most sweetly of the angels: 'The princes
of Juda are their leaders, the princes of Zabulon and the princes
of Nephtali.'[13] Their princes or leaders are here aptly given
names, the interpretation of which corresponds to the trinity
of theological virtues, without which no man can be saved,
that is to say faith, hope and charity. For Juda means 'confession', Zabulon 'dwelling-place of beauty', and Nephtali
'their breadth'.[14] Now according to the apostle it is impossible
to please God without faith,[15] and so with the heart we believe
unto justice, and with the mouth confession is made unto
salvation,[16] for the just man liveth by faith,[17] and confession
perishes from the dead man as though he were not; therefore
whosoever confesses, liveth. This faith and confession, like
mother and daughter, are nourished and stimulated by the
princes of Juda, leaders of the elect just entering upon the way
of justice, so that these may believe and confess that our Lord
Jesus Christ, the Son of God, is both God and man, and may
not fear to confess him before men, should the time come for
their faith to be put to the test. The word 'confession' does not
always imply accusation, often enough it means 'praise'. For
example, when he from whom all sin was far removed said:
'I confess to thee, Father . . .',[18] he was expressing praise, not
self-accusation.

(Ch. 3).   Let us now see where the princes of Juda lead us.
To be sure it is from faith to hope, that is from one virtue to

another,[19] as it were from the territory of Juda into the land of
Zabulon; the latter we have to traverse under the guidance of
the princes of Zabulon in order to reach the land of Nephtali,
for it is only through hope that we can arrive at charity, and
under no other leadership save that of our angels. Should
someone ask what connection there is between Zabulon and
hope, I would answer that there is such a close connection
between them that hope cannot exist where there is not a
dwelling-place of beauty, that is to say, Zabulon; for hope presupposes faith, by which the hearts of the elect are in fact
purified, and through faith Christ dwells in our hearts.[20] Is that
not indeed a dwelling-place of beauty, where he abides at
whose beauty the sun and moon marvel,[21] and on whom the
angels desire to gaze?[22] Whence also the apostle says: 'Know
you not that the temple of God is holy, for that is what you
are, and the Holy Spirit dwells within you?'[23] The Father,
however, cannot but be present where we have proof that both
the Son and the Holy Spirit dwell, and so it follows that where-
ever we find an abode of the whole Blessed Trinity, there is a
dwelling-place of beauty.

Thus the princes of Zabulon lead us in hope, so that we have
no cause to fear,[24] as far as the land of Nephtali, which is
interpreted 'their breadth'. By this I understand the broad
commandment, that is charity, which, once perfected, casts out
fear.[25] But the princes of Nephtali have to lead us to that, as it
falls within their province, for it is the especial task of the order
of seraphim to kindle and nourish love of God in the hearts of
all; their very name indeed signifies this function, for 'Seraphim' means 'burning' or 'kindling'. So we read in Isaias 6:
'There flew towards me one of the seraphim, having in his
hand a burning coal which he had taken with a pair of tongs
from the altar, and he touched my mouth.'[26] Commenting on
which, St Gregory says: 'In this saying of the prophet we are
given to understand that the spirits who are sent on a mission
receive their name from the office which they fulfil.'[27]

(Ch. 4). My opinion would, however, appear to be contra-
dicted by what Denys the Areopagite together with St Gregory
and other doctors hold to be true, namely that angels from the

highest orders are not sent, seeing it is written: 'Thousands of thousands served him, and ten thousand times a hundred thousand attended him.' [28] St Gregory explains this passage as follows: 'It is one thing to serve, and another thing to attend some one; those who are sent with messages to us serve God, but those who attend him enjoy such intimate contemplation that they are never sent out on external missions.'[29] My answer to this is that although the highest orders of angels always remain in heaven, yet they fulfil their functions through others, the highest indicating to those who hold a middle rank what is to be done, and these in their turn informing those below them, and so in a sense they are all ministering sons, sent to minister to those who are to enter into the inheritance of salvation.[30] Those angels who act through others appear to effect things themselves, and the lesser angels, who in fact carry out the tasks, are even named after these functions. For example, the angels who are sent by the seraphim to enkindle the hearts of the elect with divine love are themselves called seraphim; those sent by the cherubim to instruct the ignorant are called cherubim, and so on with the rest.

I ought not, however, to affirm anything of this sort as a certainty, nor have I any desire to do so, for different people think differently about the matter. Even St Gregory emphasizes the fact that he is not stating anything authoritatively when he says: 'Though we learn from various places in Scripture that some things are done by the Cherubim and others by the Seraphim, and it is said that these are angels who are sent by superior spirits and so named after the latter, we do not wish to state as a fact anything of which we have not manifest proof.'[31]

(Ch. 5).   Since, however, it is the more general opinion that only angels of the lower orders are sent to us, I would like to suggest yet another interpretation of that saying of the apostle, taking it in this way: all the ministering sons of the orders deputed for external missions are sent to minister to those who are to enter into the inheritance of salvation, and there is not one of them who may not be sent, if God sees that our welfare demands it. Thus the apostle does not include all the orders but all the individual angels of the lower orders. Both interpretations are to be found in the Second Book of Sentences, d. 10, ca. 6.[32] Confession and beauty are in his sight to serve him, as do the princes of Juda and Zabulon, but holiness and magnificence are in his sanctification, reposing like the princes of Nephtali.

These, then, are like gods among men:

> Of God's own Church these princes great
> Triumphant lead the ranks that fight.
> In heaven's court of high estate,
> Upon the world they shed true light.[33]

Assisted by them:

> With fervent faith the saints endure,
> While hope, unquenched in darkest hour,
> And perfect love of Christ ensure
> Their triumph over Satan's power,[34]

for they accompany us when we sally forth to meet the assaults of the demons, and in the day of battle they form a rampart round the house of the Lord. Their care for us in life is such that even in death they are not separated from us.[35] On the contrary, they lead us from death to life, and if we have to pass through fire and water, because some inflammable material such as wood, hay or straw remains in us,[36] they go with us, so that when we have been purified and are released from the heat of the fire (for none can escape from its heat), they may take us to the place of refreshment.[37]

(Ch. 6).   These angels, I repeat, dear unto both God and man, although not compassed about with infirmity, are nevertheless appointed to act on man's behalf in matters pertaining to God. They offer gifts and prayers for sin,[38] showing wonderful consideration for our toil and sorrow, although themselves far removed therefrom. They sympathize with one, console another, and aid with salutary doctrine those in ignorance and error.

Whatever blessings God bestows, whether in the way of giving his people knowledge of salvation unto the remission

of sins,[39] or of warding off danger, curing infirmities, and curb-
ing the malice of evil spirits, he does all by the hands of the
angels, with the sole exception of those works which belong to
the divine husbandman, the Trinity, alone. Such are the creation of heaven and earth and of souls, the justification of sinners
and remission of sins, a clear reading of the wills of all, the
sudden infusion of divine love into any heart, knowledge as to
who are to receive a crown and who to be condemned to the
flames, foreknowledge of all future events, promotion of the
growth of the word of God amongst those who hear it, and
other similar operations, about all of which, however, since I
do not wish to make any rash statement, I will leave it to
learned theologians to dispute.

(Ch. 7).   For the rest, it is through our most noble patrons,
the angels, that God daily works out the salvation of men
throughout the whole world, even the islands afar off,—on
one of which I myself dwell—and in the distant sea.[40] It is true
each day proclaims the word to another, and each of us may
carry another's burdens,[41] yet we believe that such things are
impossible without the help of angels. Knowing as they do
what is pleasing in the sight of the Lord, they work upon the
dispositions of men, and dispose their acts in such a way that
their charges may find favour with him.

Although they have no share in those works which are
entirely due to divine power alone, since these surpass the
angelic nature as well as our own frailty, and belong solely to
the divine husbandman, the Trinity, yet the angels must not
on that account be held by us in low esteem. We ought rather
to love them, because in matters outside their competence they
pray to the Lord that he who is mighty will do great things for
us,[42] and in the case of anything they can do, they do it, as soon
as they perceive it is God's will.

They are so powerful that no evil spirit, nor all the diabolical
spirits together, can resist them, and there is no power of darkness that can snatch out of the hands of any one of them a soul
dying in a state of grace. There is then no other people comparable in grandeur to the human race; none other has gods

which draw nigh to it as our angels stand by us[43]; and though in fact they are not gods, since there is only one God, nevertheless the gods of the pagans are not to be likened to them.

The angels are by nature so full of good-will that they love men who neither know nor love them, but who walk like fools in darkness, not repaying the love of those who watch over them while they sleep. Their love for us far surpasses even that of a mother, for during our life-time they are our guardians and attendants, brethren and fellow-citizens[44]; it is they who bear our souls to heaven and present our prayers to God, right noble warriors that they are of the eternal king, and comforters in our distress. I would not indeed blame anyone for loving his own special angel more than any other heavenly citizen. They do indeed deserve our heartfelt love, seeing that they are so much concerned for us that they watch over us continually in this life and conduct us to heaven in the next.

(Ch. 8). *The author now addresses his own angel.*

I believe that one of this august company has been assigned to me, and though I have never beheld his beauty, I have learnt from experience that he is jealous for me with the jealousy of God.[45] When I would have followed after my unlawful loves, he barred my path so that I might not lay hold of them, and thus when I was courting death it fled from me, thanks, I am convinced, to him who loved me in a more wholesome way than ever Adam did Eve.[46] And since he has never yet allowed me to yield to any woman, I will henceforth call him the guardian of my purity. If it please him, I have something now to say to him.

Whoever you may be, to whom the task of watching over me has been committed, you have favoured me with many a benefit, for often, but for you, my soul would have made its abode in hell.[47] Without a doubt you have frequently saved my body from destruction, and delivered me from the evil hour[48]; therefore will I praise you for the wonderful things you have done for me, and now I would make open acknowledgement of some of the instances in which you have brought me assistance and comfort.[49]

Once, when I was only eight years old, a leaning wall gave way and would have crushed me as it fell, if you had not swiftly caught me up and carried me fifteen feet away from the scene of the ruin. I could not possibly have jumped so far by my own strength at that tender age. On another occasion when I was walking carelessly on a plank bridging the river Cherwell, I was very nearly drowned. I had completely lost my balance and was on the point of falling in, when you suddenly lifted me up and set me upright on my feet; after this I was able to pass confidently over the water, which I had feared would prove insupportable.

(Ch. 9). How often would I have fallen into a pond or down a well, had you not placed your hand upon me, and had your right hand not saved me![50] How often when hewing wood with axe or hatchet[51] would I have maimed myself, had you not turned aside the implement as it struck, and thus averted the danger! How often you have saved me from pusillanimity of spirit and a storm, what I feared never coming to pass at all, what I dreaded never happening![52] How often would my eyes have been put out by an arrow flying in the daytime or by some contrivance confronting me in the dark,[53] but you diverted the course of the shaft and prevented me from losing my sight. How often you have taught me in my ignorance, brought me back when I had taken a wrong turning, roused me when I was all too ready to go on sleeping, consoled me when I was sad and overcome with grief, steadied me with the thought of death and the last judgement when I was dissipated with laughter and foolish joy, healed me when sick; in short whenever human counsel or aid have been of no avail, you have come hastening with all speed to my assistance. What return can I make to you for all you have rendered unto me?[54]

Let me for my part indeed love you, my venerated protector, since I cannot enrich you with material things, for you stand in no need of any I possess, and no gift of mine can profit you,[55] save that of a chaste and humble life. These are the two things which your soul loves above all, for chastity is akin to the angels, and the poor in spirit are dear to you. The opposites of these virtues provide the devil with his chief suggestions, and he has had the greatest success with them in his warfare against the human race. You hold conversation with those who are chaste and humble.[56]

(Ch. 10). Remember, O venerated master, when you stand in the sight of God, to speak well for me and to turn away his indignation from me.[57]. Although I have often behaved irreverently in your sight and, rejecting your advances, have acquiesced in the devil's suggestions, I am sorry now that I did not follow your promptings or carry out your desire concerning good actions. I beg of you, kind spirit, not to requite me according to the ingratitude with which I have often caused you confusion and frequently caused you to depart in sorrow, if indeed it is permissible to attribute such feelings to angels. Since even when you are doing things for me you are ever standing before God,[58] pain and sadness cannot come near you, and because wherever you go you move in God, your countenance cannot change,[59] beholding as you do unceasingly the face of the most high Trinity.

For after Jesus and Mary, you, together with the saints I especially love, are my only refuge. You have become the helper and guardian of my soul, and, because it trusts in you, you will not desert it, neither will you betray it into the hands of the enemy, nor forget it unto the end.[60] When my last day comes and my life here is finished, O my angel, receive my soul cleansed from all sin, and bear it up on high to see God face to face.

Since, however, where justice is concerned angels are wont to be jealous with the jealousy of the Lord and to cast down those who aspire after lofty heights, my angel says to me: 'You know not what you ask. Can you drink the chalice and eat the bread of which Elias partook before setting out for Horeb, the mountain of God?'[61] My answer is: 'I can do all things in him that strengtheneth me.'[62] (Ch. 11). But I beg of you, as you are not speaking plainly now but are as it were repeating a proverb, tell me what this parable means.[63]

You reply: 'Water is a symbol of humility, bread of charity, and the mountain is the house of the Lord for whom the angels yearn. It is of the nature of water to seek the depths and flee from the heights, for the streams will flow down through the midst of the mountains, that the valleys may abound with corn.' This means that the humble will have abundant strength from Christ, who resists the proud and gives grace to the humble.[64] Just as a table without bread is a needy one, so absence of charity is ruin to the soul, for the soul walks by love, and the man who does not love abides in death.[65] The mountain denotes the house of the Lord, of which it is written: 'Come, let us go up to the mount of the Lord and the house of the God of Jacob.'[66] So from all these things take this short lesson to yourself: be humble and love, so as to be able to see God in his house. What I have said will have shown you what sort of offerings are worthy of God. Without these two things it is impossible to be saved.

Since I cannot go up to the mountain of the Lord except I eat this bread and drink this water, I beg of you, kind spirit, to approach God on my behalf and obtain that such bread may never be lacking in his servant's wallet. May his flagon never run out of water, for bread cannot be made without this, since it is made out of flour and water, after which it must be cooked with fire, which stands for the furnace of tribulation, whence it is written: 'As gold is tried in the furnace, so the just are put to the proof of tribulation.'[67] And again: 'The man who amasses virtues but has not humility is like one who carries dust in the face of a wind.'[68] Fortified in this way, may I proceed to the mountain of the Lord, there to cry out in admiration with the prophet: 'How great is the abundance of thy sweetness, O Lord, which thou keepest hidden for them that fear thee!'[69]

To this sweetness of the blessed may the Lord, the King of angels bring us![70] Amen.

Notes to Meditation addressed to the Angels

1. Ps. xxx, 20.   2. Cf. Ps. lxxix, 18; Wis. xvi, 20–1.
3. Cf. Ps. xc, 12.   4. I Tim. i, 17.
5. Hymn *Lux ecce surgit aurea* (Lauds of Thursday).
6. Cf. Ps. lxxxix, 2.   7. Cf. Prov. viii, 24, 27.
8. Cf. Job xxxviii, 7.   9. Cf. Ps. viii, 6–7.
10. Cf. Responsory *Congratulamini mihi* (Easter Monday).
10a. Cf. I Pet. iii, 13.   11. Eph. vi, 12.

12. Cf. I Cor. x, 13; Mt. vi, 13.   13. Ps. lxvii, 28.
14. *Glossa Ordinaria in h. l.*
15. Heb. xi, 6.   16. Rom. x, 10.   17. Gal iii, 11.
18. Mt. xi, 25.   19. Cf. Ps. lxxxiii, 8. 20. Eph. iii, 17.
21. Responsory *Ipsi sum desponsata* (feast of St Agnes).
22. I Pet. i, 12.   23. I Cor. iii, 16–7.
24. Cf. Ps. lxxviii, 53.   25. I Jn. iv, 18.   26. Is. vi, 6–7.
27. St Gregory, *Homilia XXIV in Evangelia*; PL 76, 1254.
28. Dan. vii, 10.
29. St Gregory, *op. cit.* PL 76. 1254.
30. Heb. i, 14.
31. St Gregory, *op. cit.* PL 76, 1254–5.
32. Peter the Lombard, *Liber II Sententiarum*; PL 192, 673.
33. Hymn *Aeterna Christi munera* (Matins of Apostles), verse 2.
34. *Ibid.* verse 3.   35. Cf. II Kings, i, 23.
36. Cf. I Cor. iii, 12.
37. Cf. Ps. xviii, 7; Ps. lxv, 12. 38. Heb. v, 1.   39. Lk. i, 77.
40. Jer. xxxi, 10; Ps. lxiv, 6.   41. Cf. Ps. xviii, 3; Gal. vi, 2.
42. Cf. Lk. i, 49.
43. Cf. Deut. iv, 7, and sermon of Corpus Christi Matins attributed to St Thomas Aquinas.
44. Cf. Responsory *Super salutem* (*Processionale Monasticum*, p. 263).
45. Cf. II Cor. xi, 2.
46. Cf. St Bernard, *Sermo XX super Cantica*; PL 183, 868.
47. Ps. xciii, 17.   48. Ecclus. li, 3.   49. Ps. lxxxv, 17.
50. Ps. cxxxviii, 5; cxxxvii, 7.   51. Cf. Ps. lxxiii, 6.
52. Ps. liv, 9; Job iii, 25.   53. Cf. Ps. xc, 6.   54. Ps. cxv, 12.
55. Cf. Ps. xv, 2; Mt. xv, 5.   56. Cf. Prov. iii, 32.
57. Offertory *Recordare* (feast of Seven Sorrows B.V.M.), formerly a versicle of the Offertory *Recordare* (22nd Sunday after Pentecost); cf. Jer. xviii, 20.
58. Cf. Lk. i, 19.   59. Cf. I Kings, i, 18.
60. Cf. Ps. cxviii, 114; xii, 1.   61. Cf. Mt. xx, 22; III Kings xix, 8.
62. Phil. iv, 13.   63. Cf. Jn. xvi, 29; Mk. iv, 10.
64. Ps. ciii, 10; lxiv, 14; Jas. iv, 6.
65. I Jn. iii, 14.   66. Is. ii, 3.
67. Cf. Prov. xxvii, 21; Ecclus. xxvii, 6.
68. Ps-Gregory, *In VII Psalmos Poenitentiae*, iii, 3; PL 79, 569.
69. Ps. xxx, 20.   70. Cf. 12th Blessing at Matins.

5*

Meditation addressed to Abraham and David

(Ch. 1). If a man wishes to study the virtues of our fore-fathers, and delights in the exploits of men of renown, let him turn to the holy men of the Old Testament, those patriarchs and prophets, who in their own day pleased God and were accounted just![1] Although the Church does not celebrate the days on which they died as feasts, since all of them went down to Limbo, yet their memory will not perish and their names will be remembered from generation to generation.[2] For it is right that those who have gone to share the joys of the angels[3] and whose names are written in the book of life should live on in the memory of man.[4]

It seems to me that they deserve to be venerated by us all the more, since we know that before the law was given or the hour of grace had come, they performed deeds which we are scarcely worthy to admire. What counsel of perfection do we find now in the Gospel which we do not read of their having fulfilled, for even when there were only two brothers in the whole world, one of them died the death of a martyr? Then we have Elias who was a virgin and Moses a doctor of the people. Does not the whole world at this very day receive the clearest possible instruction from the example of those men from whom the Church took its origin, and from whom Christ was descended according to the flesh, he who is God most blessed for ever?[5] But it was to Abraham and David alone that the promise was made. To the one it was said: 'in thy seed all nations shall be blessed',[6] and to the other: 'I shall place one of thine own offspring upon thy throne.'[6a] I intend therefore to pass over all the others, and to address first Abraham and then David.

(Ch. 2). You, O Abraham, were indeed blessed by God most high, for you obeyed that divine voice commanding you to sacrifice the son whom you so dearly loved. And so it is written: 'God put Abraham to the proof, and said to him: "Abraham, Abraham." He answered: "Here I am." And God said to him: "Take thy son, Isaac, whom thou lovest, and go into the land of vision, and offer him to me as a sacrifice upon a certain mountain, which I shall show thee." '[7]

There we have God's command: where shall we find obedience, love, faith, fear, fulfilment of that command? Where the source of that blessing in which all nations are to be blessed, the dawn of life, the promise of redemption to mankind, where the cause of life and the destruction of death? Where find a man in whom fear of the Lord outweighs love of his son?

Show us your treasure, Abraham, manifest your virtue; give God the Father cause not to spare his Only-begotten Son[8] for your sake and that of your seed for ever. Though fear of the Lord and love of your son contend within your heart, let fear of the Lord triumph and cast out love of your son. Do what you are about to do, so that not only will all generations call you blessed,[9] but all nations will be blessed in you.[10] Raise your sword to sacrifice your son, and receive thereby promise of redemption for the human race. With whatsoever measure you measure unto God, with that same measure you will be repaid.[11] If, for his sake, you do not spare your only son,[12] he for your sake will not spare his Only begotten Son. God's goodness is such that it cannot be outdone; no one can surpass him in generosity. Abraham must not be like Adam, who for the love of a woman and the attractive appearance of an apple disobeyed God's command, though he was not himself seduced.[12a]

(Ch. 3). We shall see that the temptation which brought about Adam's fall was a slight thing indeed, if its circumstances are carefully compared with those of the temptation which might have withheld Abraham from slaying his only son. Abraham gloriously overcame the temptation. For he despised it, and by so doing he gave glory to God, helped to compensate for the fall of the angels, and forwarded the salvation of mankind.

It is clearer than daylight that the less hungry a man is, the less strong is his temptation to eat, and the better provided he is with fruit which it is lawful for him to eat from other trees, the less desire he feels to eat the fruit of one particular tree, a forbidden one at that. He has also less reason to consent to a woman's suggestion, if he has not the sting of concupiscence in his flesh. Added to that he is all the more effectively enabled to obey the divine command if his body and soul are immune from infirmity, and he has experienced the presence, the beauty and the goodness of his God.

Now Adam in fact was not hungry, for he had only lived for six hours without sin, and there was plenty of fruit for him on other trees, moreover he cannot have had concupiscence, since he was not ashamed of being naked, and added to this he was able to contemplate God and the angels, for he could both see and converse with them. In the *City of God*, book 14, chapter 17, St Augustine speaks as follows of Adam's state before the fall:

(Ch. 4).   Man lived as he pleased in paradise, as long as he desired what God commanded. He lived in the enjoyment of God, and derived goodness himself from him who is Goodness. His was a life without need of any sort, and he had it in his power to live thus for ever. There was food lest he hunger, drink lest he thirst, and the tree of life to prevent his dying of old age. His body did not contain any corruption or seed of corruption, which could have caused suffering in his senses. He feared no sickness from within, no attack from without. His body enjoyed perfect health, his mind complete serenity. Just as there was neither excessive heat nor cold in paradise, so no evil desire nor fear impaired the goodwill of him who dwelt there. He knew nothing of sadness, nor yet of senseless joy. He found continual cause for true joy in God, whom he ardently loved with charity springing from a pure heart, a good conscience, and faith unfeigned.[13]

So wrote Augustine.

How greatly to be blamed then was one who fell into sin, overcome by such a paltry temptation, when he was endowed with such noble gifts! Let us consider how differently for his part the patriarch Abraham acted. Although he was bone of Adam's bone and flesh of his flesh,[14] he had no affinity of spirit with him, for whereas Adam had despised the Lord's command, Abraham fulfilled it. The one was unfaithful, the other faithful, the one disobedient, the other obedient, the one elated, the other humble. Adam provoked God, Abraham appeased him, the action of the former brought a curse upon the world, in the seed of the latter all nations are blessed,[15] the former despised God for the sake of a fruit and a woman, the latter for God's sake was relentless towards his only son; in short, Adam and Eve brought us every evil, Abraham and Isaac are the means of all our good.

(Ch. 5). It seems to me that it is impossible for anyone to do justice to the ardent and devoted love which this most blessed man Abraham had for his God, if one takes into account the full import of his action as well as the natural instincts and diabolic suggestions which might well have dissuaded him.

Was there ever a very wealthy old man with no heir, who if he had, thanks to God's promise, miraculously begotten a son by a wife already ninety years old, would not love him more than all the riches in the world, especially if he were a well-favoured lad? And if perchance he received a divine command to offer up this son to God in sacrifice, would he not think that it was a delusion rather than a message from God? For assuredly the devil does sometimes transform himself into an angel of light[16] in order to deceive people, nor is it usual to sacrifice children to God, nor does a man easily believe what is contrary to his own wishes.

There can be no doubt at all that this man was singularly blessed, for without knowing the law, he fulfilled it, and loved the Lord God above all things, for his sake not even sparing his own son.[17] He must have had discernment of spirits, as he was able to distinguish between an angel and Satan.

O Abraham, most faithful, what did you decide to do, what did you say to yourself inwardly when you heard God's command to sacrifice Isaac?

(Ch. 6). I fancy that you must have thought in your heart: 'I do indeed love my son dearly, but I must not fear my Lord any the less. He who gave me that son by a wife advanced in years will be able, if I kill the boy, to raise him up from the dead, when he sees that I have faithfully carried out his word. I will arise by night and leave my own territory secretly, so that no one may hinder me from setting out to do my Lord's will.

Having won that battle over myself, I will set out to do it at an hour when I will meet no one to prevent me. Since it would be an easy thing to persuade a man not to kill his own son, I do not want anyone to know of my intention, neither stranger, nor acquaintance, nor servant, not my wife, and not even my son himself, until he comes to the mountain where the Lord has commanded me to sacrifice him.'

O Abraham, I exclaim, O Abraham, you contained within you the treasure with which the human race was redeemed! You are wise indeed, for in your heart lay this precious treasure which you showed to the world by your readiness to slay your own son for God's sake.

Who could ever utter praise worthy of you? Your chastity is not surpassed by the virginity of John, your faith is accounted unto justice,[18] your obedience overrules nature, fire does not undermine your steadfastness. Your hospitality is such that you entertain angels, your power of judgement such that you can discern spirits, your courage suffices to quell kings. Your prayer renders a barren woman fruitful, your hope obtains the promise, and it was your charity which caused God to become incarnate, when, by taking a human soul, he assumed flesh from your blessed seed, and the Only-begotten Son of God chose to become a man amongst men.

(Ch. 7). O Abraham, I do believe that your obedience was so pleasing to God, who chose to become man for your sake, that it outweighed the displeasure caused him by the man who presumed to eat the forbidden fruit. For it is as noble a thing to attain salvation as it is execrable to incur damnation. This would have been so in whatever way God had wrought the redemption of mankind; how much the more seeing that God became man and chose to redeem us through the agony of the Cross from the power of the wicked spirits in a way which is immeasurably great, surpassing as it does the understanding of every mind and exceeding every capacity for love.

O happy sin of Adam and praiseworthy obedience of Abraham which together merited to obtain such and so great a Redeemer,[19] sprung from no other stock but from the seed of Abraham! Isaac too was no less favoured, for he, the righteous son of a righteous father, born of a blessed one and blessed himself, offered no resistance to his father and did not recoil when the hour of immolation came, but acted in accordance with the likeness of that Son whom he prefigured, who for our sake was made obedient to the Father even unto the death of the Cross.[20]

(Ch. 8).   From his line came David, beloved of God, both king and prophet, and a man whom God found according to his own heart.[21] To him too, as I said before, the promise was made. This man's whole-hearted devotion to his God is manifested in the Books of Kings and also in the Psalms, which he sang to God with deep feeling after battle or in time of tribulation. He was evidently so much on fire with charity that he must have seemed more like an angel on earth than a man, triumphant rather than militant. He ever conversed with God by the yearning of his love, whence he says of himself: 'As the hart thirsteth for water from the springs, so doth my soul long for thee, O God.'[22] And elsewhere: 'Alas that my sojourn is prolonged!'[23]

It was the very ardour of this love, bearing him ever God-ward, that made him, in a higher degree than all the other prophets, an apt instrument of the Holy Ghost. His words are so wise and full of meaning, so fraught with hidden mysteries, that the more I ponder them, the more abundant fruit I reap from them, and there is no other part of Holy Scripture which I relish so much as the words of David, the royal harper and prophet.

(Ch. 9).   There is an astonishing thing which I have found with regard to these words, but I cannot explain it fully here; however, I will just mention it. Whatever I happen to be doing, I always seem to find David's words a help. They teach us facts, make us firm of purpose, inform our conduct, compose our thoughts, banish depression, solve our problems and teach us about the Scriptures. Assiduous meditation on them cleanses a man completely from all blindness of heart, and, just to mention something still more remarkable, any comedian, out

to raise a laugh in his audience, would find passages from the
psalms, did he but know them and care to make use of them,
which would enhance even his performance, though to debase
such sacred mystic words to such profanities would be no
slight sin.

Moreover it should be noted that the story of David's life
is of great value to the Church, serving as it does both as a goal
for those running their course and as a pattern in accordance
with which beginners in the way of justice may reform their
whole life. If you are an adulterer or murderer, then follow
David's example, for he was both; do not despair, but do
penance and say: 'Have mercy on me, O God, according to
thy great mercy.'[24]

(Ch. 10). If you are an honest man, let David be a warning
to you not to trust over much in your rectitude, for he was an
upright man and yet he had a terrible fall; be little rather in
your own eyes, as he was. For when he had already been
anointed by the prophet as God's chosen king of Israel, and
after he had killed a lion and a bear, and slain a giant, after
taking the foreskins of the Philistines to Saul, after wreaking
great slaughter amongst the Philistines and fighting a number
of battles, he called out to his persecutor: 'Whom are you
after, O King of Israel, whom are you after? You are hunting
down a dead dog and a solitary gnat.'[25] What an unspeakably
humble man, and how wonderful the humility of such a great
man, for although he was pre-eminent in every virtue amongst
his contemporaries, he thought himself the least of all. How
could he have had a lower opinion of himself than he had, and
which he expressed in a psalm: 'But I am a worm, not a man,
the reproach of men and an outcast from the people.'[26]

On account of these and similar incidents David was found
to be a man after God's own heart, for even if humility equal
to his is to be met with in others, it has never been known in a
man of such position. Humility is praiseworthy in a servant,
still more so in one who has authority, but in a king humility
such as his is altogether unheard of. If anyone should ask:
'Why should it be a great thing for a king to humble himself
before one of like rank?' I answer: 'It is a great thing indeed

for a king to humble himself, but far greater still for him to
call himself a dead dog and a gnat; there can be no question
about the humility of a man who when once cursed by a
servant bore it patiently, and said: "The Lord has sent him to
curse David." [27]

(Ch. 11).   No one, I think, can fully realize how great this
man's glory is in the salvation of the Lord.[28] As king he was
exceedingly humble, he had a wonderful love for his persecutor, for it is said of him in II Kings xix: 'Thou lovest
them that hate thee'[29]; he was a contemplative even when
engaged in warfare or oppressed by tribulation, he grieved
most bitterly over the death of those who hated him, and was
so merciful that when the Lord delivered into his hands one
bent upon putting an end to his life, he would by no means
slay him, the man whom he was to succeed as king.[30] This
makes it clearer than daylight that he was far removed from
ambition or anger, seeing that he would not take vengeance on
his enemy just because he knew that the latter was occupying
the throne which belonged to him himself, and which would
pass to him on the king's death.

David then may well be said to have been a man after God's
own heart, both because of his unprecedented humility, his
incomparable devotion, his continual meditation on God, and
the most ardent love for God which ever burnt in his heart.
He would not have called the Lord's commandments 'more
desirable than gold or precious stones and sweeter than honey
and the honeycomb'[31] had he not loved them. Thus too in
another psalm he says: 'How I have loved thy law, O Lord;
all day long it is the subject of my meditation.'[32] And in another
verse: 'I have loved thy testimonies more than gold and
topaz.'[33] Or again: 'My portion, O Lord, I have said is to
keep thy law',[34] which means: 'I say that it will be my portion,
O Lord, to be able to keep thy law.'

(Ch. 12).   Since, however, love of God is the fulfilment of
the law,[35] it follows that one who was so careful to keep the
law must have loved him greatly. Have regard then, O David,

king and prophet, and you, Abraham the patriarch, to the plague and misfortunes which beset us. Towns which were formerly well populated have been reduced to desert places by the death of the citizens, and in many a district in England there is not one left for a thousand, nor two for ten thousand. O you who have had such a sublime calling, say to God: 'Let thy wrath cease now, O Lord, from thy people and thy holy city. Remember thy testament, O Lord, and say to the angel that chastises us: 'Let thy hand cease now, lest the whole land be laid waste and thou cause every living soul to perish.'[36]

God will not refuse what you ask, for he is your son, as it is written: 'The Son of David, son of Abraham',[37] and you are holy ones of the Lord, worthy to obtain what you request. Again we read in Scripture that God shows especial mercy on your account, for the psalmist says: 'The mercies of the Lord I will sing for ever',[38] and in Mary's canticle are the words: 'He hath received Israel his servant, being mindful of his mercy, as he spoke to our fathers, towards Abraham and his seed for ever.'[39] Implore mercy then for those who need mercy, for whatever you agree to ask for on behalf of men here below will be granted, if you beseech the Father in the name of the Son, who liveth and reigneth with the Father and the Holy Ghost, world without end. Amen.

Notes to Meditation addressed to Abraham and David

1. Ecclus. xlvi, 16.   2. Ecclus. xxxix, 13.
3. Cf. Responsory *Iste sanctus* (Common of Confessor-Bishops).
4. Phil. iv, 3.   .   5. Rom. ix, 5.   6. Gen. xxii, 18.
6a. Ps. cxxxi, 11.   7. Gen. xxi, 1–3.   8. Cf. Gen. xxii, 12.
9. Cf. Lk. i, 48.   10. Cf. Gen. xii, 3.   11. Cf. Lk. vi, 38.
12. Gen. xxii, 16.   12a. Cf. I Tim. ii, 14.
13. St Augustine, *De Civitate Dei*, lib. xiv, c. 26; *PL* 41, 434; cf. I Tim. i, 5.
14. Gen. ii, 23.   15. Cf. Gen. xxvi, 4.
16. Cf. II Cor. xi, 14.   17. Rom. viii, 32.   18. Cf. Gen. xv, 6.
19. Cf. *Exsultet* (Holy Saturday Liturgy).
20. Phil. ii, 8.   21. Cf. I Kings xiii, 14.   22. Ps. xli, 1.
23. Ps. cxix, 5.   24. Ps. l, 1.   25. I Kings xxiv, 15.
26. Ps. xxi, 7.   27. Cf. II Kings xvi, 10.   28. Cf. Ps. xx, 6.
29. II Kings xix, 6.   30. Cf. I Kings, xxiv.
31. Ps. xviii, 11.   32. Ps. cxviii, 97.   33. *Ibid.* 127.
34. *Ibid.* 57.   35. Wis. vi, 19; Rom. xiii, 10.
36. Cf. Responsory *Recordare* (Matins of 4th Sunday after Pentecost) and I Par. xxi, 11–16.
37. Mt. i, 1.   38. Ps. lxxxviii, 1.   39. Lk. i, 54.

Meditation by the same author addressed to St. John the Evangelist

(Ch. 1). O St John, apostle and evangelist, most dear unto God, singled out by our Lord for your purity and loved beyond the rest,[1] who can utter words befitting you, and not falling short of what your inestimable dignity and outstanding merit demand?

If I give you the title of apostle, everything will bear out the fact that you in very truth are such. If I call you an evangelist, have you not earned that title too, since your epistles reveal you as an apostle, and your gospel proves you to be an evangelist? If I hail you as a martyr, who will not rejoice at such a title, seeing that you endured boiling oil, drank poison, underwent scourging with the other apostles, and were banished to Patmos for the sake of Christ? Shall I declare you to be a doctor, for who is it that instructs Christians and refutes those heretics who assert that before Mary Christ did not exist? Who but you, O glorious Saint, you who declare to us the Word in the beginning?

Were I to call you an angel, it would not be enough and I needs must add that you were in very truth shown to be an angel of angels, when delegated as ambassador and messenger of the supreme judge to the seven angels of Asia. The angel realized this when he would not let you adore him, since he was but your brother, fellow of those holding the faith of Christ Jesus.[2] If I choose to call you a virgin, the whole Church will be able to bear reliable witness to what I say, for it was as a virgin that you were singled out by our Lord, and called away by him from your wedding.[3] Thereupon you were happy to exchange the delights of sensual pleasure for the sweetness of divine love, and this we may well believe gave rise to a hundred times as much joy in your heart as ever sensuality would have caused pleasure.

(Ch. 2). If I want to assert that you were the friend of God, we read that you were loved more than the rest. If gifts and confidences go to make up friendship, to whom have God's secrets been revealed if not to you, who are so holy? And who was given Christ's mother to be his own mother but you, who are so chaste? Rejoice in your good fortune, undying praise is yours, for you became the Virgin's son and so the brother of the Redeemer.

If I would extol you as a prophet, who amongst the ranks of the prophets is more outstanding than you, our own St John, author of the renowned Apocalypse, which sets forth the state of the universal Church from the beginning of the world until the end of time, and contains nearly as many hidden mysteries as words?

What shall I say about you, who are so dear to God? I can certainly declare with full confidence that of all the blessings that fall to the lot of any saint you receive from the just judge to be stored up in your heart good measure, heaped up, shaken together and overflowing.[4] But woe and alas, eloquence fails, the tongue falters, and the mind's eye is blinded by the splendour of this sublime pillar of light.

If Christ's words are true, or rather because they are true, they are essentially real and must needs be fulfilled; you are the son of Christ's mother and the brother of our Redeemer, and that not merely by a single title but by Christ's repeated word, as it is written: 'Woman, behold thy son,' but to the disciple, 'behold thy mother.'[5]

(Ch. 3). Who could presume to compare you with any other, seeing that you recline trustfully on the bosom of the Only-begotten Son of God, that treasury of all wisdom and knowledge? Your tomb is found to contain manna instead of worms and corruption, you are especially appointed by Christ to be the guardian of the temple of purity and the sanctuary of the Holy Spirit, and your dignity and grace surpass those of all others save of our Saviour and his venerated Mother alone. Moreover, I would dare to say that as long as you were born of a woman, you were equal to John the Baptist, but since you became the son of the Virgin and brother of Christ, there is none left to be compared with you.

You are then chosen from amongst the elect, the holiest of saints, pattern of chastity and mirror of virginity, friend of God and servant of Jesus Christ. Every Christian is bound to love you above all others after Christ and his mother, for it stands to reason that the one who was dearest to Christ should be dearest also to Christ's faithful followers. In your loving kindness bow down your ear to our prayers. Grant us to perform joyfully whatever Christ most wants us to do, and never allow us to commit such acts as Christ has forbidden, so that we may die in peace with him.

(Ch. 4). By these sweet privileges which you alone have deserved to receive from God, grant that anyone who devoutly meditates on these praises in your honour may never be overthrown by Satan our enemy, nor suddenly overtaken by an evil death. Keep him from destruction by sea or land, and let him not fall a prey to his enemy; may no backbiter harm his reputation, no invader seize his goods, no adversary prevail over him, and may the necessaries of life never be lacking to him. Let no tempest injure him, and no calamity overwhelm him; may he never be at a loss for an answer, never intoxicated nor glutted with food; may he never be tripped up by any diabolical snare nor deluded by the devil in dreams at night. Let not fire or water approach to hurt him, nor anything either attractive or repellent cause him to deviate from the right way; grant that he may not fall into mortal sin on that particular day, nor incur eternal damnation by dying in a state of sin. May he feel love increasing within him to such an extent as to love the maker of all above all else; in short let no disaster overtake him, and after death let him not suffer the fierce pains of fire, but when the judge comes to take his place in wrath, may he be allotted a crown and enter with his judge into everlasting joy. Amen.

Here the meditation ends.

Notes to Meditation addressed to St John the Evangelist

1. Cf. Responsory *Valde honorandus est* (feast of St John Evangelist).
2. Apoc. xix, 10.
3. Cf. *Vita et Acta S. Iohannis* (Mombritius, *Sanctuarium*, ii, 61).
4. Cf. Lk. vi, 38.   5. Jn. xix, 26–7.

Meditation by the same author addressed to the most
Blessed Cuthbert, Bishop of Lindisfarne

O Cuthbert, God's priest and splendid servant, appease for
us your king, who has taken you to be one of his own citizens,
calling you out of darkness into his wondrous light.[1] Father,
be mindful of your own flock, which has no confidence in its
own merits, and suffer not to succumb to the dangers of mortal
life, those to whom you have left your holy body as a pledge.

> Shepherd art thou and protector to those all who love thy
> name,
> But a weapon of destruction, where men flout thy lawful
> claim.
> Shining dove from heaven winging, told thy coming
> here on earth;
> Thou foreknewest well her offspring, ere the cow
> brought calf to birth.
> Slipping from thy hands a volume fell into the rippling
> sea,
> But an otter did return it, dry despite the waves, to thee.
> Like a ship upon the ocean at thy word a stone did
> float;
> Thee, and with thee too thy mother, brought from
> Scottish shores a boat.
> When the bishop's feathered favourite was by hateful
> malice slain,
> Thou, to please its saddened master, brought it back to life
> again.[2]

What shall I say about you, O holy Cuthbert, our patron,
bishop dear to God? I cannot do justice to your miracles, for
their number defies human computation, and no more can I
describe your holiness. Every year you work new miracles,
and as long as you lived, you never ceased to please Christ. As
you yourself once said: 'I never mind being wakened; on the
contrary, the caller does me a favour, because he enables me
to throw off the inertia of sleep, and either think or do something
worth while.'[3] Your great love for God and continual

contemplation of him eventually took such possession of your heart, that you fled the companionship of other men, and rejoicing to be deprived of human intercourse, went to Farne, and remained there for nine years alone.[4]

I should like to know, God's dear saint, what work you did or what virtue you manifested that pleased Christ so much that he adorned not only your life but your very death itself with miracles, punishing so severely those who wronged you, that you are accounted by all a second Lawrence. I have no doubt that you had some special quality, in regard to which none was found like to you, who kept the law of the most high as you did,[5] and it is that quality which I propose to investigate, if I can, in this meditation. I humbly beg of you to open the ear of my understanding, that I may know what it was. I can think of no better way of finding out than by having recourse to the actual words of your own last farewell to your brethren. . . . [6]

Notes to Meditation addressed to St Cuthbert

1. Cf. I Pet. ii, 9.
2. These verses reproduce material from the so-called Irish life of St Cuthbert, *Libellus de Ortu S. Cuthberti* (*BHL* 2026) and Reginald of Durham's *Libellus de admirandis virtutibus S. Cuthberti* (*BHL* 2032). They are probably out of their original order and the text is partially corrupt; possibly they represent the verses which later adorned the stained-glass window in Durham cathedral, described by the *Rites of Durham* (ed. Fowler, p. 3). For other hymns to St Cuthbert cf. Dreves, *Analecta Hymnica*, xii, 101–3, xxviii, 90, xi, 1032–4, etc.
3. St Bede, *Vita S. Cuthberti*, c. xvi (ed. B. Colgrave, *Two Lives of St Cuthbert*, 212).
4. Cf. Colgrave, *op. cit*. Introduction, 7–8.
5. Cf. Ecclus. xliv, 20.
6. The text ends here in the MS. in the middle of a page ruled with lines throughout. St Cuthbert's exhortation to his monks referred to is reproduced below from St Bede's Life of St Cuthbert, c. xxxix (ed. B. Colgrave, 283–5):
   'Always keep peace and divine charity amongst yourselves; and when necessity compels you to take counsel about your affairs, see to it most earnestly that you are unanimous in your counsels. But also have mutual agreement with other servants of Christ and do not despise those of the household of the faith who come to you for the sake of hospitality, but see that you receive such, keep them and send them away with friendly kindness, by no means thinking yourselves better than others who are your fellows in the same faith and manner of life. But have no communion with those who depart from the unity of the catholic peace, either in not celebrating Easter at the

proper time or in evil living. And you are to know and remember that if necessity compels you to choose one of two evils, I would much rather you should take my bones from the tomb, carry them with you and departing from this place dwell wherever God may ordain, than that in any way you should consent to iniquity and put your necks under the yoke of schismatics. Strive to learn and to observe moſt diligently the catholic ſtatutes of the fathers, and praꝭise with zeal those rules of regular discipline which the divine mercy has deigned to give you through my miniſtry. For I know that, although I seemed contemptible to some while I lived, yet after my death you will see what I was and how my teaching is not to be despised.'

Walter Berschin's recent ſtudy of this passage in *St Cuthbert, his Cult and Community* (1989) emphasises the differences in ſtyle and vocabulary from those of Bede: this points to it being, as is claimed, the words of Herefrith rather than the words of Bede.